Heroes of
Fighter Command

SUSSEX

Rupert Matthews

COUNTRYSIDE BOOKS
NEWBURY BERKSHIRE

First published 2007
© Rupert Matthews 2007

COUNTRYSIDE BOOKS
3 Catherine Road,
Newbury, Berkshire.

To view our complete range of books,
please visit us at
www.countrysidebooks.co.uk

ISBN 978 1 84674 036 7

Spitfires of No 65 Squadron (FZ – 65)
(From *Spitfire – The Story of a Famous Fighter*,
by Bruce Robertson 1960)

Designed by Peter Davies, Nautilus Design
Produced through MRM Associates Ltd, Reading
Printed by Cambridge University Press

*All material for the manufacture of this book was
sourced from sustainable forests.*

CONTENTS

Preface 4

Introduction 7

Chapter 1   War Comes to Sussex 15

Chapter 2   The Battle of Britain Begins 35

Chapter 3   Chucking Out the Book 55

Chapter 4   Invasion Alert 72

Chapter 5   Messerschmitt Month 90

Chapter 6   Into the Night 105

Chapter 7   Back to France 124

Chapter 8   On the Back Foot 149

Chapter 9   The Invasion of Europe 171

Index 190

Preface

Strangely enough, through all the bombings and doodlebug and rocket attacks, the only time I can ever remember feeling frightened was one night in 1940.

For once and surprisingly, the air raid sirens had not sounded. It was a pleasant dry evening when we and our neighbours stood out in the darkness quite late chatting and wondering why the Germans had not come. Should we go to sleep in our beds or would that be a waste of time and in an hour or so should we need to jump up and go down under the stairs or – horrors – into the air raid shelter?

There were the usual jokes about had Jerry forgotten that there was a war on and should we try to phone them up and say had their alarm clocks not gone off and did they not know it was eleven at night and time to get into their aeroplanes?

But then we gradually noticed in the far southeast a red glow on the horizon. In those days of total blackout, what could it be?

We walked across a field to slightly higher ground where the view was not obscured by trees. All the sky in the direction of London was red.

London was burning.

The grown-ups fell silent. There were no more jokes. If we could see the glow of the fire from so far away, then extensive areas of London must be going up in flames. What would remain in the morning? Would all the government offices be destroyed? What about Churchill and other members of the War Cabinet? Were they being killed? Who would be left to tell us what to do and how to fight the war?

Everyone was very upset. After a while we turned and walked home and went to bed. No wonder the planes had not come over us. They were all concentrated on London.

In the morning we eagerly listened to the radio news. They neither told us until several days afterwards exactly where the raids had been nor how much damage had been done. Why do the enemy's reconnaissance work for them? But the bulletins did say that in spite of heavy raids, the government was safe. Churchill was alive and promising retaliation.

Churchill was still there for us. That was all we wanted to know.

I remember many years later, when Churchill died at a grand old age and the war was long behind us, I still could not help feeling desolation and wondering, 'Who is there to look after us now?'

As if an old man of 92 or whatever it was could have done anything in a more modern world. But who else was there who was so much on our side?

So my mother told me about just one of her experiences as a girl in wartime Britain. It was to save London and the rest of Britain from such awesome destruction that Fighter Command had been created. Even as London was burning that night, the men of RAF Fighter Command were learning the skills of nightfighting so that they could protect civilians such as my mother from attack.

And, although she did not know it then, her future husband, and my father, was wearing an Air Force blue uniform at the time. His squadron fought long and hard through the Battle of Britain. I grew up listening to stories from my parents about the war and what it had been like from their two very different perspectives. When the chance came to write this book I leapt at it. I wanted to learn so much more about those brave Few who risked, and tragically often lost, their lives. So for my father, for his pals – whether they returned or not – and for all the others who served in the RAF, I am proud to write this book.

As the title suggests, the main subjects are the men who fought in Fighter Command in Sussex during the war, their actions and their exploits. For those readers with a wider interest in the RAF who want to learn more about the airfields and unit histories I can do no better than advise you to purchase *Sussex Airfields in the Second World War* by Robin Brooks, also published by Countryside Books, which makes a fine companion volume to this.

Of course, such a book cannot possibly be the work of just one person. I would particularly like to thank Squadron Leader Andrew Smith for his help in making contact with various serving and retired officers and men of the RAF. There are two excellent air museums in Sussex, both of which have been helpful to me. The Tangmere Military Aviation Museum, Tangmere Road, Tangmere, has its website on www.tangmere-museum.org.uk/ and is open throughout the year. It is a must for anyone interested in the RAF and has a vast array of exhibits in a purpose-built museum. The Robertsbridge Air Museum is run by local enthusiasts and is open only on the last weekend of each month and selected bank holidays. It boasts a wide variety of exhibits and an impressive dedication to recovering and preserving locally-found artefacts. It is located on a farm off the A21, half a mile north of the village. Both museums are well worth a visit. I must also thank David Andrews for access to his photographic archive.

I also thank Paul Lazell for permission to use photographs taken by his father during his extensive career in the wartime RAF. Copies of these are available from Paul for a modest fee on paulsdadsphotos@aol.com. My thanks, too, to Brenzett Aeronautical Museum for their help and for permission to use photographs of their exhibits in this book. The museum stands just over the county border in Kent, off the A2070, and is well worth a visit; full details can be obtained on their website www.brenzettaero. co.uk/. They have some particularly fine interactive exhibits for children of all ages.

I have made every effort to track down the copyright holders of material that I have used, but if I have missed anyone out please accept this as a genuine mistake and contact me so that matters can be put right in any future edition.

Finally I would thank my mother for her inspiration, my wife for her patience and my daughter for her constant questions.

INTRODUCTION

To the pre-war military planners, Sussex was never intended to be a major base for the RAF and its fighters. It was confidently predicted that any war with Germany would be fought out in a similar fashion to the last one. As in the First World War, long lines of trenches would stretch across northern Europe with British and French armies on one side, and German armies on the other. Much of the RAF would be in France, behind the front line, flying patrols over the battlefields. Those aircraft that flew from Britain would be concentrated in Kent and East Anglia, either flying bombing raids to Germany across the North Sea or fighting off raids coming the other way.

It did not turn out like that, of course, and Sussex found itself in the front line for five long, arduous years. Yet, the face of Fighter Command in Sussex grew out of that pre-war thinking, so to understand what follows it is necessary to look briefly back to the very birth of Fighter Command on 14 July 1936.

When it was formed, Fighter Command had 15 squadrons, plus three auxiliary squadrons. The government had authorised an expansion to 35 squadrons and was providing phased payments to make this possible by 1942. There were nine stations, of which only one – Tangmere – was in Sussex.

All the aircraft flown by Fighter Command were biplanes with open cockpits, such as Bulldogs, Demons and Gauntlets. These aircraft could just about top 200 mph and were armed with twin machine guns. Such aircraft performed only marginally better than had the fighters of World War I. At a time when Germany was producing bombers able to fly at 230 mph and bristling with six machine guns, these fighters were outclassed.

Fortunately the first commander of Fighter Command was a former World War I fighter pilot with a deep interest in and appreciation of technical advances. Air Marshal Sir Hugh Dowding was 54 years old and had a reputation for austerity that earned him the nickname of 'Stuffy' throughout the RAF. When Dowding moved into Fighter Command headquarters at Bentley Priory, his first move was to draw up a wish list of what he wanted.

Fortunately for Dowding, two modern fighters were already in development. The first was the Hawker Hurricane, the second the Supermarine Spitfire. Both were sleek monoplanes with retractable undercarriages, able to fly

Air Marshal Sir Hugh Dowding was head of Fighter Command when war broke out in 1939. He had been the commanding officer since 1936 and had moulded the air defences of the nation very much according to his own ideas. His statue stands outside the church of St Clement Danes in the City of London.

at above 320 mph and armed with eight machine guns. Experience would show that each had its strengths and weaknesses, but in 1936 the important thing was that they could fly fast enough to catch the most modern bombers and had the firepower to bring them down. They would, however, be slow to arrive. The Hurricane entered service in 1938 and the Spitfire in 1939. When war broke out some squadrons still had the old biplanes.

As the number and quality of squadrons expanded, Dowding saw the need for extra airfields. Quite apart from the need for more space, there was a pressing necessity for dispersal. There was no point concentrating all of Fighter Command's strength in a few well-known locations where an enemy air force could bomb them to destruction. The fighters had to be scattered around at different airbases to make it harder for the enemy to hit them when they were vulnerable on the ground.

It must be remembered that Dowding and his staff officers had been assured by the army and the French that any future war would see German bombers flying from airbases in Germany or, at most, in Holland. Nobody seriously expected the German army to get any closer to Britain than that. So while fighter airbases were being hurriedly bought or built elsewhere, Sussex remained rather quiet.

The civilian airfield at Ford was bought in 1938, but only for training purposes. When war broke out it was still a training base and did not become a fully operational fighter base until September 1940. Thorney Island, on the Hampshire border, was built from scratch in 1938, again as a training base. In 1939 it was transferred to Coastal Command as a base from which to fly anti-U-boat patrols. It would later be used by Fighter Command, though only on a temporary basis.

Westhampnett was built on a stretch of flat farmland in 1938 as an emergency landing ground for battle-damaged aircraft. It was upgraded to a Fighter Command base in 1940. Shoreham was another civilian airfield commandeered for war use, this time in August 1939. Administratively, Shoreham was operated from Kenley in Surrey until 1944, when it was transferred to Tangmere. Friston was a civilian airfield used on a part-time basis by the RAF from 1936 onward. It was taken over in 1940 and in 1942 rebuilt to be a proper fighter airfield.

So as war approached, Sussex had only one proper fighter base: Tangmere. As the demands of war changed many more would be built, but not yet.

Meanwhile, Dowding had another problem to solve. He would soon have modern fighters spread across the country they had to protect, but he still

A squadron of Hurricanes in formation over Sussex, probably at Tangmere, as this is a pre-war photograph.

A squadron of Hurricane pilots race for their machines 'somewhere in France'. The exercise was staged for the benefit of press photographers in October 1939 to show the readiness of RAF units in France.

needed a way to locate the incoming bombers. Even as late as 1936 the only way to locate an aircraft from the ground was to listen and look for it. Massive concrete 'sound mirrors' were built in Kent facing the North Sea, which could, in theory, catch the sound of distant air motors long before the unaided human ear. And the Observer Corps, part of Fighter Command, had keen-eyed staff with binoculars along the coast.

It was not enough. If Fighter Command did not locate enemy aircraft until they were within sight of land it was unlikely that the fighters could be scrambled to meet them in time to catch them. Fortunately the RAF had been encouraging the development of a device known then as Radio Direction Finding (RDF) but which would later become famous as radar. The development had been approved in 1935, but until 1938 the boffins – as scientists were known in the RAF – were unable to get the apparatus to work reliably. The first radar stations were set up in Kent and Essex, looking out across the North Sea at Germany, and the chain was not extended to Sussex until the early months of 1940. Put simply, the radar stations were designed to locate enemy aircraft formations at a distance from the British coast, the Observer Corps were tasked with tracking them once they were over Britain.

As Fighter Command grew, Dowding had to spend time sorting out its organisation. By 1939 he had divided his command into five distinct groups, each under the control of an Air Vice Marshal and having a fair degree of operational independence from Fighter Command HQ at Bentley Priory. The far north of England and Scotland were covered by 13 Group; the Midlands, East Anglia and Wales by 12 Group; the South West by 10 Group, while 11 Group covered London and the South East. Sussex came under Air Vice Marshal E. Gossage and 11 Group, with its headquarters at Uxbridge in Middlesex.

But as the countdown to war began, Dowding suddenly found all his careful preparations put at risk. In April 1939 the British and French military held a conference to discuss detailed plans of how to behave if war broke out with Germany. New and more accurate estimates of Luftwaffe strength were available, and they badly worried the French. France had expanded her air force in the previous two years, but not to any great extent. They feared being overwhelmed by the modern and numerous aircraft of the Luftwaffe and demanded that the British send four squadrons of Hurricanes immediately war broke out, with a further six squadrons to be sent to France within three months.

A pre-war photo of Hurricane fighters flying in formation. The Hurricane Mk 1, shown here, was armed with eight 0.303 machine guns and was much praised as being a stable gun platform in a dogfight.

Sir Keith Park, Dowding's deputy, who attended the conference, prevaricated. He knew that Dowding was deeply worried by the fact that Germany had over 1,400 bombers able to fly from Germany to bomb London and other cities in eastern England. Dowding believed that he would be stretched to defend Britain as it was and had been relying on the French themselves to defend France. In the event the politicians stepped in. They instructed Dowding that he would have to send four squadrons of Hurricanes to France as soon as war broke out, but assured him that these aircraft would be used only to protect the British army in France from air attack. The question of the further six squadrons was left open.

On the day war broke out, RAF Fighter Command had 39 squadrons, two of them stationed in Sussex at Tangmere. The two Sussex squadrons, Nos 1 and 43, both had Hurricanes. Neither of them was to be sent to France immediately. Instead they were to form a second line of defence in case any German bombers got past the front line fighter squadrons in Kent and East Anglia.

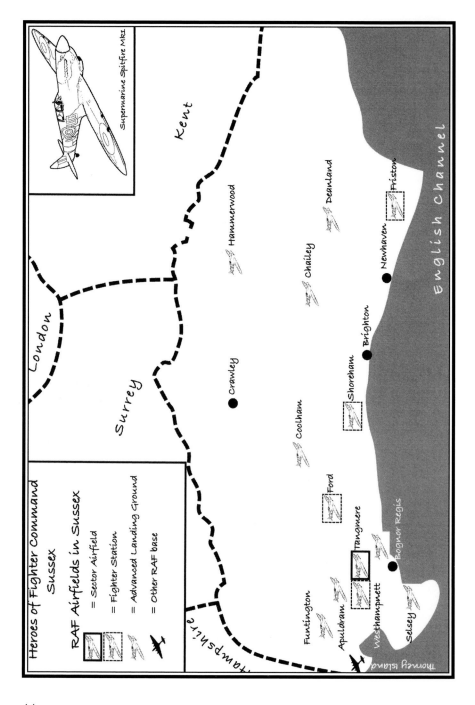

Supermarine Spitfire Mk1

Kent

London

Surrey

Hampshire

English Channel

Heroes of Fighter Command Sussex

RAF Airfields in Sussex

= Sector Airfield

= Fighter Station

= Advanced Landing Ground

= Other RAF base

Hammerwood

Deanland

Chailey

Newhaven

Friston

Crawley

Brighton

Shoreham

Coolham

Ford

Tangmere

Bognor Regis

Funtington

Apuldram

Westhampnett

Selsey

Thorney Island

Chapter 1

War Comes to Sussex

Sussex got off to a flying start when war was declared on 3 September 1939, despite its designated role as a second line of defence. Within hours of the news breaking that Germany had invaded Poland, the head of Fighter Command, Sir Hugh Dowding, was in Tangmere. He had come to see Squadron Leader P. 'Bull' Halahan, the commander of No 1 Squadron, and he had a lot to say.

No 1 Squadron was one of those whose Hurricanes were earmarked for service in France. Preparations had been made weeks before to transport the squadron staff and all its ground equipment to France. Now Dowding came to give 'Bull' Halahan some very specific instructions personally. He was not, Dowding said, to risk his aircraft or men unnecessarily. There was to be no fancy flying, just workmanlike missions. Above all, Halahan should expect no reinforcements. He had his twelve aircraft and twelve pilots, which was what Dowding had been forced to promise the French. No more

Widely known as 'Bull', Squadron Leader P.J. Halahan led No 1 Squadron from Tangmere to France and back again. Before he left for France he received private orders from Dowding not to waste men or aircraft needlessly.

One of the most outstanding fighter pilots in Sussex when the war broke out was Peter Townsend. He went on to be awarded the Distinguished Flying Cross and Bar in 1940 and the Distinguished Service Order in 1941. After the war he was involved in a famous romance with Princess Margaret.

would go to France. Every fighter was going to be needed at home to protect British cities and British bases from attack.

Halahan did not record his reaction to this news. He led his squadron out to France to await the German onslaught.

That left only No 43 Squadron at Tangmere, though they were soon joined by No 92 Squadron. One of the pilots of No 43 Squadron had already gained a reputation for superb flying skills, but was famously shy on the ground. This was Flying Officer Peter Townsend, who had joined the RAF in 1935 and served on bombers for a while before joining No 43 in September 1938. Townsend achieved his first victory in the air on 3 February 1940, when he shot down a Heinkel 111. He went to see the survivors of the German crew in hospital next day and after the war stayed in touch with one of them, Karl Missy.

No 43 Squadron was later transferred to the far north of Scotland to defend the naval base at Scapa Flow. While there Townsend shot down two more German bombers, one after a prolonged chase and combat that had taken him far out over the North Sea. In May 1940 he was put in command of No 85 Squadron and moved to Martlesham. There he was himself shot down into the sea, but was rescued by a patrol craft.

In August 1940 Townsend and No 85 Squadron moved south again, this time to Croydon. By then the Battle of Britain was raging. On one day the squadron was scrambled and vectored in by radar on a German formation which turned out to be 250-strong. Undeterred by the odds, Townsend led his squadron to the attack and ten Germans were shot down. Townsend was awarded a bar to his Distinguished Flying Cross (DFC) for that action. Soon afterwards Townsend was shot down again, and this time was out of action for a year.

In February 1944 he was appointed as equerry to King George VI and it was while at Buckingham Palace that he met and fell in love with Princess Margaret. By 1953, when her sister was celebrating her coronation as Queen Elizabeth II, the romance had become clear to everyone close to the pair, and word was leaking out to the public. The problem was that Townsend was divorced. While this did not preclude him from marrying into royalty, it would have caused some social problems and difficulties with the Church of England, of which Margaret's elder sister was head.

In the event the couple did not marry. Townsend left the RAF in 1956 to take up a career in journalism and later acted as an advisor on the making of the classic movie *The Battle of Britain*. In 1959 he married a Frenchwoman and moved to France, where he died in 1995.

Meanwhile, in September 1939, Dowding had to face up to the task of defending Britain. According to the latest intelligence reports, the Luftwaffe had 4,161 combat-ready aircraft, of which about half were bombers able to reach Britain from Germany. To face them Dowding had 1,099 fighters – of which only about 800 would be available at any one time, owing to maintenance and other issues. In fact the Luftwaffe had 4,100 aircraft in total. A good number of these were transport or reconnaissance aircraft and only around 1,600 were front-line bombers. Even so, the odds were against Fighter Command if the Germans launched an all-out attack on Britain.

That did not happen. Although London air raid sirens went off less than an hour after war had been declared, the cause was a French aircraft that failed to send out identification signals, rather than a German raid. In fact the Luftwaffe was heavily engaged in Poland and only a few patrols were being flown over the Western Front.

The first German air raid on Britain did not take place until 16 October, when a formation came up the Firth of Forth to try to bomb naval ships anchored in the bay. Two German bombers were shot down by Spitfires based nearby. No German bombers came even close to Sussex, so the Hurricanes and Blenheim fighters at Tangmere did little more than fly routine and practice patrols.

That practice had received some indirect help on 24 September when a French Morane 406 fighter shot down a Messerschmitt Bf 109. The German aircraft came down relatively intact, certainly enough survived to allow the boffins to study it. They quickly found that it carried only four machine guns. This made it a 'D' model and was misleading, as the 'E' model with its two 20 mm cannon was then being introduced and would soon be present in large numbers. Nevertheless, the crashed aircraft did give the RAF a fair idea of the 109's abilities.

The winter of 1939–1940 was severe, with the heaviest snowfalls for 20 years. The government prevailed upon Dowding to despatch two more fighter squadrons to France. He responded by sending across two squadrons equipped with biplane Gladiators, fit only for very local defence of airfields and the like. He was still determined to keep his modern aircraft in Britain.

Throughout the bad weather the expansion of Fighter Command continued. New aircraft were rolling off the production lines and new pilots were being trained – many of them civilian pilots being taught the skills of war flying. Tangmere was expanded to be a four squadron airfield, with three Hurricane

The wreckage of the first German aircraft to be brought down on British soil. This Heinkel He 111 had been on a mission to bomb warships off the Scottish coast when it was shot down.

The cover of a German magazine published in 1939. It shows a Luftwaffe bomber crew member set against a map of Britain. The article inside boasted of the Luftwaffe's might and Britain's claimed weakness.

A Blenheim Mk 1 circles over a burning German merchant ship in the North Sea in March 1940. The fastest fighter in the RAF when it was introduced in 1937, the Blenheim was outclassed by German fighters in 1940 and soon moved out of the front line.

squadrons and one equipped with Blenheims. These Blenheims were twin-engined, long range fighters that had been designed to accompany bomber formations on raids into enemy territory. It would soon become clear that they were no match for the German fighters and by the spring of 1940 the Blenheim Mk 1 was to be withdrawn from front line service.

In February 1940, 11 Group, of which Tangmere was part, received a new commander. Gossage was transferred to be Inspector General of the RAF, while his place was taken by Air Vice Marshal Sir Keith Park, Dowding's deputy at Bentley Priory. At the same time the South African Air Vice Marshal Sir Christopher Quinn took over 10 Group. Dowding himself was due for moving on, but he was kept in position as the government felt that this was no time to take on a new head of Fighter Command.

By this time, Dowding had been forced to send out to France several new fighters to replace those lost through the wear and tear of operating from temporary airfields in a foreign country. He did not like it, but so long as it did not involve depleting the strength of Fighter Command in Britain he accepted the situation. It was now clear that Hitler was waiting for the bad winter weather to lift before making his next move. Everyone expected that to be an invasion of France, possibly marching his armies through Belgium, in April or May.

When the Germans did spring into action on 9 April 1940 it caught nearly everyone by surprise. They did not invade France, but Norway and Denmark. The invasions had been ordered because Germany's vital supplies of iron ore from Sweden were shipped down the Norwegian coast and past Denmark. Without iron, Germany could not fight a war and Hitler was determined to safeguard those supplies before taking on Britain and France. The news that British warships were laying mines off the Norwegian coast had led Hitler to make the move. Denmark was overrun quickly, but Norway held out longer. The British sent an expeditionary force to Narvik to aid the Norwegian defenders and Dowding was forced to contribute two squadrons. In the fighting that followed both squadrons were wiped out, though several personnel were evacuated by sea.

The campaign not only cost Dowding two squadrons, it also gave the Luftwaffe bases in southern Norway much closer to Scotland than its bases in Germany. Dowding began to consider moving forces from Tangmere to Montrose, but events overtook him.

On 10 May 1940 the Germans launched their long expected attack in the West. As had been expected the offensive opened with attacks on Belgium, but Holland too was invaded. Using parachute troops to seize key bridges and concentrated panzer columns to punch through defences, the Germans advanced quickly. Guessing that they were sweeping across the Low Countries to outflank the massive defences of the Maginot Line on the Franco-German border, the Allied High Command advanced their armies into Belgium. The British Expeditionary Force (BEF), with Dowding's valuable Hurricane squadrons, went north to link up with the Belgian army just east of Brussels. They were accompanied by four more Fighter Command squadrons, bringing the total in France up to ten.

Winston Churchill in September 1939 when he was in government as First Lord of the Admiralty. Before the war he had championed the cause of a much enlarged RAF, but had been largely ignored by the then government.

It proved to be a disastrous move. The German advance into Holland and Belgium had merely been a feint. The main German attack was delivered further south, through the Ardennes mountains and over the key Meuse river at Sedan. Once over the Meuse on 14 May there were no natural obstacles between the panzers and the sea. The German tanks raced forward and by 20 May the Germans reached the Channel coast near Abbeville.

As the panzers swept on, the new British Prime Minister, Winston Churchill, called an emergency Cabinet meeting to decide what should be done. Dowding was in attendance to give his views. About 200 British fighters had been lost in France up to this date by one cause or another. Dowding now thought that France was as good as beaten and decided that he had to keep his remaining aircraft in Britain. After others had spoken to outline the general military situation, Churchill outlined the matters for decision. When he came to the request from the French government

23

The beach at Dunkirk, photographed from a Royal Navy ship waiting offshore to pick up British soldiers. Fighter Command flew hundreds of sorties to Dunkirk to try to keep the Luftwaffe away from the beaches.

General Lord Gort, VC. In 1939 he was appointed to command the British Forces in France. It was Gort's decision to ignore the protests of his French colleagues and retreat to Dunkirk that allowed the British army to escape annihilation in 1940.

that more British fighters should be sent to France, he asked Dowding to comment. Dowding outlined his views, and then handed Churchill a graph showing the losses of Fighter Command to date, and how those losses would continue into the future. 'Prime Minister,' Dowding said, 'if we carry on like this for another 14 days we shall not have a single Hurricane left in France or in this country.' The doomladen statement was followed by a grim silence while Churchill studied the graph. Then Churchill nodded, no more fighters would go to France.

The entire BEF and much of the French army were north of the panzers and cut off from their supply lines. Lord Gort, the commander of the BEF, reckoned that he had enough food to keep his men going for a week, but only enough ammunition for five days of fighting. He ordered his men to retreat to Dunkirk in the hope that the Navy could evacuate them. The French objected and protested, but offered no viable alternative and merely insisted that the British should attack instead of retreating. The retreat went on.

On 26 May 1940 the evacuation began. The Navy famously commandeered hundreds of small yachts and pleasure craft from around the English coastline to take men off the beaches while larger destroyers and ships used the port. But all this effort would have been in vain if the Luftwaffe had been free to bomb the evacuation fleet in the Channel. That was where the RAF, and the squadrons of Tangmere, came in.

Tangmere's Hurricanes flew their first missions to the Continent on 10 May 1940. These early flights were to try to keep the Luftwaffe off the

The assembled pilots of No 601 Squadron at Tangmere in 1940. The squadron arrived at Tangmere in February 1940 and flew many missions out to Dunkirk from the base.

retreating Allied armies. By 25 May the main objective was to protect the evacuation fleet off Dunkirk and the British troops around Dunkirk itself. The fighters were close to the limit of their range, allowing them only a few minutes' fighting time before they had to turn round and return. Nevertheless they did manage to frustrate the majority of the Luftwaffe attacks. It was unfortunate that most air combats took place out of sight of the men on the beaches, leading many soldiers to bemoan the fact that the RAF had not been there when needed.

One of the RAF pilots shot down at this time had his photograph published and story reported in the press. As was then the usual practice, his name was not given, though he was a Flying Officer out of Tangmere. The pilot came down south of Antwerp on 14 May, behind German lines. This particular pilot spoke a smattering of French, enough to make himself roughly understood by the Belgian farmer he met an hour later. He borrowed a suit of clothes from the farmer, who advised him to tell people that he was a seasonal worker from the south of France, which would explain his terrible accent.

Duly disguised, the pilot set off to walk west, in the hope of reaching the British lines. As he walked, he picked up the news that the Allies were retreating headlong before the panzers. He attached himself to bands of Belgian refugees, repeating his story about being from France, to avoid being too conspicuous. On the fifth day he got a ride in a truck along with a group of Belgian refugees. The truck was stopped by a group of German infantry and the pilot thought his luck had run out. But the Germans were too intent on stealing the truck to bother checking the identity papers of those riding in it. He began walking again.

On the tenth day of walking the pilot began to hear gunfire and saw a black cloud hanging ominously in the air to the northwest. He did not know it, but he was approaching Dunkirk. Next day the number of German soldiers increased dramatically and it was clear he was coming up to the front lines. Time and again he had to hide to escape detection. As evening drew on he found himself faced by an open stretch of pastureland dotted by German soldiers and artillery. Suddenly the chatter of machine guns high overhead signalled the start of a dogfight as a squadron of Spitfires attacked a force of Heinkels heading for Dunkirk. All the German soldiers gazed upward. Seizing his opportunity, the pilot began to squirm forward.

Once past the Germans he was faced by a canal. As dusk came on he swam across, and was promptly arrested by a patrol of French soldiers. They passed him on to their captain, who sent him back to a senior officer.

A contemporary photo of the unnamed Sussex fighter pilot who was shot down behind German lines in Belgium, but managed to get back to England by way of the Dunkirk evacuation. He is here shown in the clothes he borrowed from a farmer to get past German soldiers.

That French officer sent the pilot under armed guard to a British outpost under suspicion of being a German in disguise. The pilot quickly convinced the British that he really was a downed RAF pilot and so was evacuated back to England and his squadron.

Also in action over Dunkirk was Squadron Leader the Hon. Max Aitken, son of the famous newspaper proprietor Lord Beaverbrook, head of the *Express* publishing empire. On 28 May he was leading his section of three Hurricanes when he spotted a formation of twelve Heinkel 111s heading away from Dunkirk, no doubt having dropped their bombs. Aitken led an attack in which he sent one bomber plunging toward the ground with one wing on fire and smoke pouring from the other. A second bomber was also sent down by a pilot of No 601 Squadron. Much to Aitken's chagrin, the Intelligence Officer at Tangmere listed the two only as 'damaged' since none of the Hurricane pilots had seen them actually crash.

Next day Aitken and his section were back in action and this time they were determined to make no mistakes. They came across a force of 15 Heinkel 111s and a similar number of Junker Ju 87 Stuka divebombers, all escorted by a squadron of Messerschmitt Me 110 fighters. Despite being outnumbered, the Hurricane pilots attacked on this occasion sending three Germans crashing from the skies. Aitken himself accounted for one Heinkel and one Stuka. They made sure they saw the enemy aircraft crash this time, and duly reported the fact to the Intelligence Officer back at Tangmere.

Just before these two actions, for which Aitken was awarded a DFC, he and his father had been drawn into a controversy that was then raging through Fighter Command. In 1936 a form of bullet-proof glass had been developed. This was made up of several layers of very thick glass, sandwiching between them thin layers of plastic, and was fitted to the front windscreen of the Hurricanes and Spitfires. It was positioned so that it and the massive engine would, between them, shield the pilot from any bullets coming from the front. Since it was at that date envisaged that most combats would be against bombers, it was believed that any incoming fire would come from the bombers the fighter was attacking.

Hurricane pilots sat in a wicker chair with a perspex canopy above them and the thin fuselage walls on either side and below. Thus they were completely unprotected from bullets coming from any direction except head-on. The early air combats soon showed that German bombers operating over France were always escorted by fighters. These fighters usually sought to get on the tail of the British aircraft and open fire from behind. Clearly what was needed was some form of armour to protect the backs of the pilots.

RAF Bomber Command already had such armour fitted as standard. It took the form of a sheet of 4 mm-thick hardened steel that sat just behind the pilot's seat. Unfortunately it was too heavy and the wrong shape simply to be slotted into a fighter. Development of a version for fighters was put in hand, and this was being fitted to all new aircraft by March 1940. The programme to fit the new seat armour to existing aircraft was proceeding at the painfully slow rate of 20 per week.

When Lord Beaverbrook heard of what was happening, he got one of his staff to knock up a version that would fit a Hurricane and had it driven down to Tangmere to be fitted to Max's aircraft. Up to this date Max had a reputation as something of a playboy. He

Squadron Leader the Hon. Max Aitken, son of the famous newspaper proprietor Lord Beaverbrook, saw action over Dunkirk and during the Battle of Britain flying out of Tangmere. He is shown here in a 1940 photograph taken when he was awarded a DFC. He survived the war as a much decorated hero.

was enormously rich and strikingly good looking. Before the war he had been a noted socialite on the London scene and even when war broke out took every opportunity to pop up to London to see his rich pals and girlfriends.

But when the workman arrived to fit the armour, Max Aitken refused point blank to have anything to do with it. He sent the man packing; then he phoned his father to explain that he and his squadron pals were a tight-knit group of fighting men who faced death daily. It would be deeply unfair, he said, to take advantage of his father's wealth in this way. Lord Beaverbrook was taken aback, but sat thinking. A few days later the workman was back at Tangmere, but this time he had enough pieces of armour plate to equip every aircraft in the squadron.

Max Aitken went on to be awarded the DFC for his courage in battle. He ended the war as a Group Captain, leaving the RAF to join his father's company. He ran the *Express* empire for many years after his father's death, but sold up in 1977 and took to yachting as a hobby. He died in 1985.

On the night of 2 June 1940 the British rearguard was hurriedly evacuated from Dunkirk. Just before dawn a destroyer cruised offshore while an officer shouted through a megaphone urging any soldiers still on the beach to come down to the sea to be taken off. Nobody came. The evacuation was over. In all 224,000 British and 95,000 Allied soldiers had been rescued. It was an incredible feat, in no small part due to the men of Fighter Command.

One of the RAF pilots sent over to France was Denis Crowley-Milling, a former Rolls-Royce engineering apprentice, who was with No 615, a Hurricane unit. They had been based south of Abbeville and so had escaped the retreat to Dunkirk. Instead the squadron had fallen back to a new temporary base near Chartres, behind the four British divisions still in France. Under the French commander, Paul Weygand, the remnants of the Allied armies now dug in to defend a new line. It was a near hopeless task, as the new front was longer than the original one but there were fewer men to defend it.

The German attack began on 5 June and broke through in the west two days later. Weygand rather unhelpfully announced to the press that 'the Battle of the Somme is lost'. At this much of the French army simply disintegrated. The ground crews of No 615 Squadron hurriedly packed up and drove back to the airfield at Le Mans. The aircraft followed by air, trying to harass the Germans as they went.

On 9 June 1940 the French government decided to abandon Paris and next day Italy declared war on France. On 11 June Churchill flew to Tours to attend a French Cabinet meeting. He sat in stony silence as Weygand blamed the British for everything; then he announced that in his opinion an immediate surrender was necessary. Prime Minister Reynaud refused, and ordered Weygand to try to hold the line of the Seine river while French gold reserves and military equipment were evacuated to overseas colonies.

But events – and Hitler's panzers – were moving faster than Reynaud or Weygand imagined. Paris fell on 14 June, Orleans and Dijon on 16 June and Besancon on 17 June. That day No 615 Squadron was moved to Nantes on the Loire estuary with orders to fly cover over the port of St Nazaire, where 40,000 British troops were gathering to be evacuated by the Royal Navy. This second, and little known, evacuation went well. The Hurricanes of No 615 kept off the few Luftwaffe bombers that tried to intervene and by 19 June only a few men were left. No 615 was ordered to fly a last patrol at dawn on the 20th and then head for England. Due to a misunderstanding, however, the ground crews evacuated as soon as the Hurricanes were in the air, unaware that the pilots would be landing to refuel and rearm before heading for England. When the pilots touched down at Nantes at mid-morning it was to find the place deserted.

The Hurricanes did not have enough fuel to get to England, and some of them needed attention before they could face the long haul north. It was then that Denis Crowley-Milling came into his own. With his engineering background he was able to show the other pilots how to refuel and rearm their Hurricanes, while he himself serviced those engines that needed attention. One by one the aircraft got off the ground and headed north. Crowley-Milling was one of the last to go. He left behind a note reading 'We have taken off for Tangmere' in case any stragglers turned up. As he raced away he passed over the leading motorised units of the German army driving into Nantes. It had been a near run thing.

One of the last RAF pilots to escape from France in 1940, Denis Crowley-Milling was known as 'The Crow' to his comrades in No 242 Squadron at Tangmere in 1940. He later attained the rank of Air Marshal and devoted his retirement to raising money for the RAF Benevolent Fund.

Back in England, Crowley-Milling stayed at Tangmere for a while, shooting down a Heinkel 111, before

A group of RAF pilots meet with their squadron Intelligence Officer after a mission in 1939 to discuss their observations and experiences. The wall behind is plastered with information on enemy bombers.

moving on to join No 242 Squadron at a base in East Anglia. He went on to have an adventurous war. As well as shooting down seven confirmed German aircraft, Crowley-Milling was shot down himself over France in 1941. He was given civilian clothes by a farmer and put in touch with the French Resistance. Moving by way of Abbeville, Paris and Marseille, Crowley-Milling eventually found himself being led over the Pyrenees to Spain. He was back in England in time to take part in the costly Dieppe Raid in August 1942, but soon after that his eyesight gave out and he ceased operational flying.

Crowley-Milling remained in the RAF after the war, rising steadily through the senior ranks to command various stations – including Hong Kong – and serving as Air Attaché in Washington before attaining the rank of Air Marshal. He retired in 1975 to devote himself to fundraising for the RAF Benevolent Fund and was made Gentleman Usher of the Scarlet Rod of the Order of the Bath. He died in 1996.

Supermarine Spitfire

Type:	Single-seat fighter
Engine:	1030 hp Rolls-Royce Merlin
Wingspan:	36 ft 10 in
Length:	29 ft 11 in
Height:	11 ft 5 in
Weight:	Empty 4,810 lb
	Loaded 5,844 lb
Armament:	8 x 0.303 machine guns in wings
Max speed:	355
Ceiling:	31,900 ft
Range:	575 miles
Production:	20,351

A Spitfire turns on its wingtip as it zooms over England for an Air Ministry publicity photograph issued in 1940.

When the Spitfire entered service it was immediately recognised as being a revolution in aircraft design. With its all-metal cantilevered monoplane design, retractable undercarriage and eight-gun armament, the 'Spit' was the most modern and effective aircraft in the RAF. Pilots recognised its easy handling and superlative combat manoeuvrability and it quickly became the favourite of RAF Fighter Command. However, its sophisticated design made it less easy to maintain than other fighters, so the Spitfire was more often unable to fly than the Hurricane. The figures given above are for the Spitfire Mk I, the standard variant during the Battle of Britain. It was later to be produced in eleven main marks, plus three naval variants, dubbed 'Seafires', and was the only pre-war Allied fighter to remain in production to the end of the war.

Chapter 2

The Battle of Britain Begins

The fall of France and the entry of Italy into the conflict profoundly altered the entire balance of the war. Italy's army may not have been of high quality, but its fleet and air force were. Suddenly the entire Mediterranean became a war zone as the Royal Navy struggled with the Italian navy and air force for control of the vital sea lanes. Closer to home, German warships and U-boats now had the use of France's Atlantic ports, putting them much closer to the convoy routes across the Atlantic on which Britain relied.

Of rather more concern to the men of RAF Fighter Command in Sussex was the fact that the Luftwaffe was now based just over the Channel instead of hundreds of miles away in Germany. Enemy bombers would no longer be coming from the east with limited flying time over Britain, they would now be coming from the south, with hours of fuel to spare. More worryingly, the bombers could be escorted by the short-range single-engined Messerschmitt Bf 109 in large numbers – not only by the less nimble twin-engined Messerschmitt 110 fighter.

Sussex was now right in the front line. Soon the RAF bases there would be in the thick of it.

But first there was a curious hiatus. Hitler had decided to occupy almost half of France, though local government in occupied areas was to be kept largely in French hands. The southern parts of the country were left to the

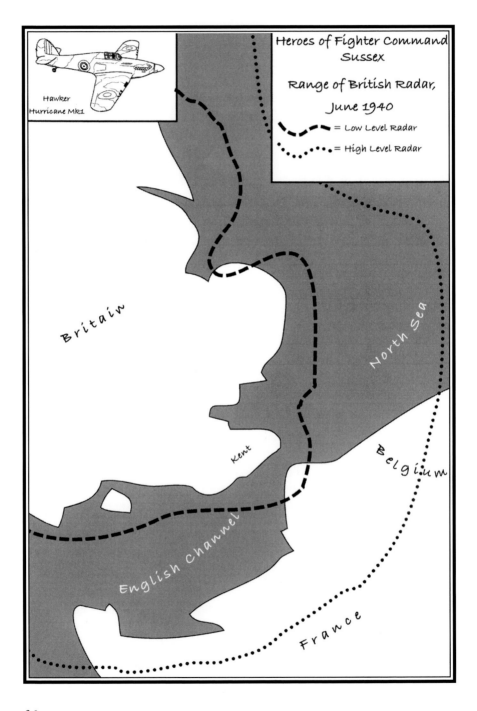

Hawker
Hurricane Mk1

Heroes of Fighter Command
Sussex

Range of British Radar,

June 1940

------ = Low Level Radar
••••••• = High Level Radar

Britain

North Sea

Kent

Belgium

English Channel

France

nominally independent French government, now based in the town of Vichy. With France crushed and occupied, Hitler seems to have thought that the war was over. He ordered the demobilisation of 35 army reserve divisions that had been called up in August 1939 and allowed leave on a rotating basis for those still mobilised. Through neutral diplomatic channels, the German government offered to open talks with Britain to discuss peace terms. Hitler declared that he was prepared to be generous. There were hints that he would leave Britain and her Empire free to pursue their traditional policies of free trade on the seas if Germany were left free to do what it wanted on the land in Europe.

But Britain had gone to war allied to France to preserve Polish independence. Churchill made it quite clear late in June 1940 that no peace could be tolerated unless it also included France and Poland. Finally, on 2 July, Hitler accepted that Britain would not make peace despite what he termed 'her militarily hopeless position'. Hitler ordered his top staff officers to prepare plans for the invasion of Britain, with a provisional date of late August.

If Hitler had been surprised by Britain's refusal to surrender, his staff were taken aback by the instructions to invade. German rearmament throughout the 1930s had been based on the assumption that the Reich would fight land-based campaigns. And between Hitler's army and Britain lay the open sea of the English Channel.

Admiral Erich Raeder, head of the navy, was sent for. He too was perturbed. Since 1935 he had been building up the German navy for a war with Britain, but had repeatedly told Hitler that it would not be ready until 1942. Even then he had envisaged a war strategy based on blockading Britain by sea, sinking convoys in the Atlantic and thus starving Britain into surrender. The German fleet had not been designed for a climactic battle in the narrow waters of the English Channel, and in any case it was not ready. Unwilling to tell Hitler the idea of invading Britain was doomed to failure because of the power of the massed guns of the Royal Navy, Raedar promised to draw up plans for getting the German army over the Channel. But he laid down as a strict condition that the Germans must have total control of the air. That put the ball firmly into the court of Reich Marshal Hermann Goering, head of the Luftwaffe.

Goering was not only supreme commander of the air force, he was an heroic fighter ace from World War I and top Nazi political leader. He gathered his senior commanders to study the problem of gaining control of the air over southern Britain, the English Channel and southern North

A group of No 43 Squadron pilots photographed at Tangmere in 1940.

Sea by late in August. They quickly realised that the key was to drive the aircraft of RAF Fighter Command from the skies. This could be done either by shooting down all the fighter aircraft in combat, or by bombing the fighter stations to destruction so that the aircraft could not operate over the invasion area.

The Luftwaffe chiefs did some calculations based on their experiences of the war in France, what their intelligence told them of the strength of Fighter Command and what they knew of the power of the Luftwaffe. They reckoned that it would take about two or three weeks to achieve mastery of the air in the areas demanded by the navy. Given that the invasion was tentatively scheduled for late August – and might well slip back to September – Goering reasoned that there was no point opening the main campaign so soon.

Meanwhile, the Luftwaffe would be sent to probe British defences, test the fighting skills of the British pilots and see how quickly the British would respond to attacks. Information thus gained would be fed into the planning process for the main air assault. Goering decided to send his men on attacks against coastal convoys and land targets close to the coast.

Pilot Officer Woods Scawen of No 43 Squadron was sent up along with five other pilots of the squadron from Tangmere to intercept a formation of Germans heading for Portsmouth. The Hurricanes attacked in the standard tactic of two groups of three each in a 'V' formation. The combat that followed ended inconclusively, though Woods Scawen sent a Messerschmitt 110 spiralling down with smoke pouring from one engine. Most of the bombers got through, but their formation had been broken up and the bombing was scattered.

Woods Scawen, meanwhile, had been separated from his comrades and was over mid-Channel at about 15,000 ft. It was then that he spotted a massed formation of around 50 Junkers Ju 87 Stuka divebombers flying straight and level away from him towards Britain. Woods Scawen reasoned that if he flew into the formation from the rear, the German rear gunners would be unable to open fire on him for fear of hitting their comrades. Once through them, he could climb steep and fast to escape the Germans' forward-firing wing guns.

No sooner had Woods Scawen thought of the plan than he put it into effect. Accelerating to high speed, he overtook the Stukas and nosed into the rear of the formation, opening fire as he did so. His target Stuka at once broke away into a dive with smoke pouring from its engine. Moving on to another target, Woods Scawen sent that Stuka into a spin. Just as he was closing on a third victim, the British pilot felt his aircraft buck and twist as the slip stream of the aircraft ahead of him struck his Hurricane. His aim spoiled, Woods Scawen pushed on to open fire on a fourth Stuka, which began to smoke. That was when one German rear gunner opened fire. The bullets

A flight of Junkers Ju 87 Stuka divebombers, of which about 6,000 were to be built. The Stuka could deliver its bombload of up to 4,500 lb with incredible accuracy. The fearsome reputation of the aircraft was enhanced by the screaming sirens fitted to the undercarriage.

splattered over the Hurricane, tearing the fuselage and wings to pieces.

With a sudden searing pain in both his legs, Woods Scawen pulled up out of the German formation and flew straight into a squadron of

A German Bf 109 fighter circles after setting fire to a barrage balloon over Bognor Regis in the early phase of the Battle of Britain.

Messerschmitt 110 fighters that had been escorting the Stukas and was now coming down to join the fight. Wounded, flying a damaged fighter and outnumbered, Woods Scawen knew he was in trouble. Fortunately the Hurricane had a speed advantage of almost 30 mph over the Me 110 and so he was able to dive away and head for Tangmere.

Bombs fall around a convoy in the English Channel while Stuka divebombers fly overhead. Attacks by Stukas on convoys provoked many aerial combats during July and August 1940.

Back on the ground, Woods Scawen's battered aircraft was attended by first aid crews, who carried the pilot off to the Medical Officer. When his blood-soaked trousers and boots were cut off they showed that Woods Scawen had not, as he thought, been hit by German bullets but by a spray of tiny fragments of metal blasted off the Hurricane by the incoming fire. 'You've got multiple foreign bodies in both legs,' observed the MO, at which Woods Scawen burst out laughing. He was still laughing when his fellow pilots bought him a drink before packing him off to hospital.

Those 'multiple foreign bodies' were thought a great joke by the fighter pilots and the story raced through Fighter Command, making it into the newspapers a week or two later. Woods Scawen was back on duty a month later, but sadly was shot down and killed in September.

Tangmere provided another story for the newspapers on 21 July 1940, but this time there was little to laugh at, though it had a more profound impact on the war. A convoy was off Bognor Regis making its way up the English Channel toward London when radar picked up a force of German aircraft moving towards it. The raiders turned out to be 40 Dornier Do 17 bombers, escorted by around 20 Messerschmitt Bf 109s and a similar number of Messerschmitt 110s.

Six Hurricanes of No 43 Squadron were available at Tangmere, so they were sent up to intercept. Led by Squadron Leader Badger, the half dozen Hurricanes adopted the standard two groups of three in 'V' formation and climbed for height. They were still 2,000 ft below the Germans when they saw them. 'Huns ahead. It's like looking up at the Piccadilly Circus escalator,' reported Badger. 'Line ahead, chaps. Let's upset them a bit.'

Badger led his section of three Hurricanes into the bombers, while Flight Lieutenant Morgan took his section up to face the Messerschmitts. Badger opened fire at around 250 yards and saw chunks flying off one Dornier before he moved on to a second, which had an engine quickly knocked out.

High above, the 110s were forming into a defensive circle, so that the forward-firing cannon of each covered the aircraft in front and its rear machine gun that behind. Morgan led his section in a steeply climbing turn to assault the circle. When he opened fire, his first burst smashed the wing of a 110, causing it to dive down toward the sea. Another Hurricane set a second 110 on fire.

Then the Bf 109s dived down to join the fray. Two got on to the tail of Morgan's Hurricane. Suddenly Morgan's cockpit canopy was covered in oil. Presuming that his engine had been hit, Morgan dived out of the fight and headed back to Tangmere with his head poked uncomfortably out of the cockpit so he could see where he was going. Badger was similarly out of the running, a cannon shell having smashed his port aileron. One by one the British fighters dropped down out of the fight and headed for home.

When they landed, the six pilots found that only one Hurricane had escaped undamaged. Bizarrely that was Morgan's aircraft. The oil that splattered his cockpit and most of the fuselage must have come from a damaged German aircraft. Between them, the pilots claimed to have damaged twelve German aircraft, but since none had been seen to crash none was counted as a confirmed kill.

An American newspaper reporter was visiting Tangmere that day and spoke to the pilots after they landed in their shot-up Hurricanes. 'How many did you meet?' he asked. 'Oh, about 40 Dorniers,' answered Badger lightly. 'Plus about the same number of Messerschmitts. Yes, must have been about 80 in all.' Odds of 80 to six

Issued by the government in August 1940, this photo shows the pilots of an unidentified Spitfire squadron 'somewhere in southern England, ready for immediate call to action'.

spoken of that casually impressed the reporter so much that he wrote up a graphic account of the combat that lost nothing in the telling. It was wired to the USA and syndicated out to newspapers across the country. With hindsight, this was the first time since the Fall of France that the American public began to think that Hitler was not going to get everything his own way.

Flight Sergeant William Franklin managed the quite remarkable feat, possibly unique, of being awarded an immediate Distinguished Flying Medal (DFM), only to be awarded an immediate Bar for an action that took place four days later. Franklin had already shot down three Germans and shared in the credit for three more when he took off with his flight on 25 June to intercept a German force over the Channel. Franklin's section was ordered to attack the 15 Messerschmitt Bf 109s flying escort. In the resulting dogfight, Franklin shot down two of the German fighters. Both aircraft were seen to crash into the sea by his comrades, so the kills were confirmed. When he got back to base the ground crew found that he had fired only 240 rounds. 'This Flight Sergeant is a determined and cool-thinking pilot,' wrote his commanding officer when making the recommendation for a medal.

On 29 June 1940 Franklin was back in the air to intercept a formation of Junkers Ju 88 bombers escorted by Messerschmitt Bf 109s. Again, Franklin was sent after the fighters while others dealt with the bombers. He got on the tail of a Bf 109, and thought that he had damaged it before it dived away. Franklin went down after the enemy fighter to make sure of it, only to see the German pull out of its dive apparently undamaged and race for France at barely 100 ft above the waves. Franklin dived down and gave chase. Tense minutes ticked by as he sought to catch up with the fleeing German. Eventually, as the French coast loomed up ahead, Franklin got to within extreme range. He opened up with a long burst and had the satisfaction of seeing the Messerschmitt stagger, then dive into the sea.

Turning for home, Franklin began climbing for height. He was about halfway back over the Channel when he was bounced by seven more Bf 109s. Now it was Franklin's turn to be the one racing for a friendly shore. He jinked and sideslipped as the Germans came down to launch attack after attack. On the fifth attack one of the Bf 109s got in front of Franklin's Hurricane. Franklin opened fire and the Messerschmitt exploded. The other Germans then gave up the chase, and Franklin got his battered aircraft back to base.

Once again his commanding officer picked up his pen to write about Franklin's 'magnificent fighting ability and success'. 'I strongly recommend him for the immediate award of a Bar to the DFM,' concluded the report.

As July slipped by, the Luftwaffe began trying a new tactic: night bombing.

A high explosive bomb bursts in a suburb of south London in September 1940. The height of the blasted smoke and debris shows that this is probably a 500 lb bomb.

The shattered tail of a Heinkel He 111 bomber stands beside bomb-blasted suburban homes.

Having, as he thought, got the measure of Fighter Command's abilities by day, Goering now wanted to test them at night. Flying by night caused problems for the Luftwaffe bomber pilots. Navigating their way to a target was difficult. They were, however, helped by the fact that they were sent almost exclusively against coastal targets, such as ports and docks. On even the darkest nights it is possible to distinguish land from sea and the shape of the coastline was enough of an aid to find the right town – though any attempts at accurate bomb-aiming were doomed to failure except on nights of a bright moon, soon to become known as a 'bomber's moon'.

For the fighter pilots sent up from Tangmere to intercept the bombers, things were even more difficult. Radar operators could vector them to within a mile or so of the enemy bomber, but the fighter pilot then had to try to spot a black aircraft against the black sky or even blacker land. Effectively, it was only if it were caught by a searchlight from the ground that the fighter pilot stood any chance of seeing the bomber and keeping it in view long enough to launch an attack.

Squadron Leader Max Aitken was on standby one night in July when radar picked up a loose straggle of night bombers heading for Southampton. He at once sprang into his fighter and took off. There was a covering of light cloud over Southampton and the searchlight crews were moving their beams slowly over the underside of the clouds. The light diffused through the clouds and silhouetted the German bombers above.

Choosing a Heinkel He 111 as a victim, Aitken dived down to attack. He opened fire at about 200 yards. Ammunition for fighting at night included a tracer every tenth bullet so that the fighter pilot could see where his shots were going. Aitken raked the German bomber from end to end, but with no discernable result. Carefully keeping the bomber in sight as it now headed out to sea, Aitken came around for a second pass. As he overshot the German bomber a second time, Aitken saw a red glow inside the fuselage. The enemy was on fire.

Aitken's altimeter was now indicating that they were dangerously low, so he climbed for height and then launched a parachute flare. The Heinkel was by now sitting on the sea, wallowing about as a column of smoke rose from the fuselage. Aitken circled while the flare burned, but he saw no sign of life or movement and no dinghy was launched. When the flared died, Aitken headed home.

That same night another night-flying pilot tackled a Junkers Ju 88. This time the bullets must have hit a bomb for the German aircraft suddenly exploded in an enormous ball of flame that grew to envelop the British fighter. The hapless pilot saw red and yellow flames surround him on all sides, licking at his cockpit canopy. Then the flames were gone and he was alone in the pitch dark sky. The entire outer covering of his aircraft was singed and the paint burned away, but the aircraft was otherwise undamaged and he landed safely.

Tangmere was, at this time, home to a squadron of Blenheim fighters. These aircraft were outclassed by the German Messerschmitt Bf 109 and were inferior to the Messerschmitt Me 110, which they resembled in having twin engines and a rear-firing machine gun in a dorsal position. By June they had been taken off daylight missions now that German bombers over Britain were escorted by fighters, but the RAF had several hundred Blenheim fighters, so they were moved to nightfighter duties, where their long range was a distinct advantage.

For hour after hour, night after night, the Tangmere Blenheims cruised over a blacked-out England waiting to be vectored toward an enemy by ground-based radar. Their exploits were sometimes reported in the press, though the names of aircrew were not given.

One Blenheim crew decided to take advantage of the dorsal gun by stalking a German bomber from below. Coming up slowly from behind, the British pilot hoped to get directly underneath without being seen. The Blenheim gunner could then open fire without the German being able to retaliate. It was with great shock that, having got into position, the gunner saw the German's bomb bay doors open as he took aim. Seconds later the bombs fell, whistling down within inches of the British aircraft. Amazingly the Blenheim emerged unscathed, but the German had escaped into the darkness.

Another Blenheim crew was luckier. They closed on a Dornier Do 17 that was illuminated by a searchlight and opened fire with the four machine guns facing forward from the fighter's nose. The German aircraft caught

Brought down 'somewhere in southern England', this Bf 109 has crashlanded almost intact. It is being guarded by RAF personnel.

An air raid siren. There were two versions of this device. This electrically powered version was usually mounted on top of buildings in towns and villages and was exceptionally loud. The smaller hand-cranked version was more often mounted at RAF bases and was still very loud. (Brenzett AM)

An RAF wheeled stretcher. These objects were frequently used to transport wounded aircrew from damaged aircraft to medical facilties. (Brenzett AM)

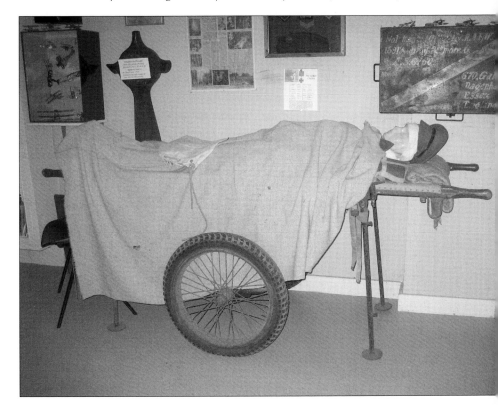

fire and began to dive. A second German bomber, not until then seen by the Blenheim pilot, turned suddenly to escape a collision and flew straight into the searchlight beam. It was then promptly shot down, leaving the Blenheim crew to celebrate having downed two Germans in two minutes.

Late one night a Blenheim crew were rather surprised to see what looked like a glittering silver road laid out over Sussex at about 22,000 ft. Although this was very close to the Blenheim's operational ceiling, the pilot decided to investigate the peculiar phenomenon. As he drew closer to the 'road' he saw it was only a few feet wide, but stretched out apparently endlessly to the west. Suddenly realising that what he was looking at glittering in the moonlight was a frozen vapour trail left by an aircraft, the pilot turned to give chase to whatever had caused it. After some time a distant black dot at the head of the trail came into sight and, as the Blenheim drew closer, the dot was revealed to be a Heinkel He 111. Minutes later it was shot down, to crashland in a Sussex churchyard among the tombstones.

Although the Tangmere Blenheim crews remained nameless in the contemporary press reports, one of them was to achieve fame not just in the RAF but in the glitzy world of Hollywood showbusiness. Tony Bartley came to Tangmere in November 1939 to fly the Blenheims, but did not achieve any combat success until after he transferred to Spitfires.

In March 1941 Bartley was moved to a training unit to instruct new pilots on combat flying in the Spitfire and in July he moved to Supermarine to be a test pilot. There he brought his combat experience to bear on the development of the new versions of the Spitfire then being worked on. Although not all his ideas could be put into practice for technical reasons, Bartley's experience proved invaluable. He also had his first brush with showbusiness when he flew the Spitfire in the movie *The First of the Few*, a biography of Spitfire designer R.J. Mitchell.

In 1943 Bartley returned to combat, commanding No 111 Squadron during the Torch landings in North Africa, and then leading that unit in the fighting that ended with the surrender of the famed Afrika Korps at Tunis. During this time Bartley shot down three Messerschmitt Bf 109 fighters and took his score up to eight confirmed kills. Thereafter he spent the rest of the war in training or staff positions, ending the war in the Palau Islands in the Pacific.

In 1947 he married the glamorous film star Deborah Kerr and was plunged into the world of showbusiness, moving to Hollywood in 1949. He then worked for CBS Films in the USA and Rediffusion in the UK, before

Hawker Hurricane

Type:	Single-seat fighter
Engine:	1030 hp Rolls-Royce Merlin
Wingspan:	40 ft
Length:	31 ft 5 in
Height:	13 ft
Weight	Empty 4,982 lb
	Loaded 6,532 lb
Armament:	8 x 0.303 machine guns in wings
Max speed:	324
Ceiling:	34,200 ft
Range:	600 miles
Production:	14,449

A pre-war photo of the Hawker Hurricane Mk 1. This was the RAF's first monoplane fighter, and the first to be armed with eight machine guns, two having previously been the standard.

The first of the low-wing monoplane fighters to enter service with the RAF, the Hurricane was a vast improvement on any other aircraft then in British service. When war came it quickly proved itself to be a reliable fighter in combat conditions. It was beloved by its pilots as a 'steady gun platform' and was frequently employed to tackle German bombers while the more agile Spitfires dealt with the fighters. The figures given above relate to the Hurricane Mk I, the version that fought through the Battle of Britain. By 1941 the Mk II was entering service with an uprated 1460 hp Merlin engine and consequent improvements in performance. This Mk II could carry a range of weaponry, including twelve machine guns or four 20 mm cannon. The Mk IIC could carry either 1000 lb of bombs or racks of rockets and was known informally as the 'Hurribomber'. The Hurricane was still in service when the war ended in 1945.

moving to Barbados to become Director of the Caribbean Broadcasting Corporation, and finally he moved to Ireland to found his own television programme production company. He died in 2001 at the age of 82.

Bristol Blenheim 1F

Type:	Twin-engined fighter
Engine:	2 x 840 hp Bristol Mercury VIII
Wingspan:	56 ft 4 in
Length:	39 ft 9 in
Height:	9 ft 10 in
Weight:	Empty 8840 lb Loaded 12,500 lb
Armament:	6 x 0.303 machine guns, nose, wing and dorsal mountings
Max speed:	278 mph
Ceiling:	22,500 ft
Range:	1100 miles
Production:	694

The Bristol Aircraft Company originally intended the Blenheim to be a civilian transport and passenger aircraft, flying the first model in 1936. However, when the RAF heard of its then impressive speed and endurance, they ordered several hundred converted to military use to give the RAF a modern fighter before the Hurricane and Spitfire, then at design stage, could enter service. The Blenheim was produced as both a fighter, to which the figures given above apply, and as a bomber. The bomber carried 1000 lbs of bombs and had only two machine guns. Fighting in France revealed the weakness of the Blenheim when faced by German fighters and it was taken out of daylight use. It was the most numerous night-fighter in RAF use until 1941, when the Beaufighter overtook it, but it remained in service for another year or two.

Successful though the pilots of Fighter Command had been during July 1940, their overall commander Sir Hugh Dowding was painfully aware that so far the Germans had been launching only nuisance or probing attacks. The worst was yet to come.

Chapter 3

Chucking out the Book

On 31 July 1940, Hitler held another top level military conference to discuss the invasion of Britain.

The army put forward a plan which envisaged the main landings taking place between Folkestone and Brighton using the 16th and 9th Armies, while the 6th Army carried out secondary diversionary landings in Lyme Bay and along the Hampshire coast. Paratroops would be used to capture Dover and Ramsgate. After four days establishing a secure beachhead, the panzers would break out to thrust north between London and Reading. They would then fan out to surround London while the infantry came up to capture the cities and towns left isolated by the panzer thrust. If that did not force Britain to surrender, the panzers would head for Birmingham and Liverpool to cut Britain in half from the Channel to the Irish Sea. Britain would surrender within six weeks of the first landings, it was predicted.

Admiral Raeder then put the naval view. He said that he could not guarantee to keep control of the entire English Channel and suggested dropping the landings at Lyme Bay. There was also the problem of transport ships and landing barges. Raeder estimated that he could gather enough to transport ten divisions at a time. Allowing for wastage and casualties, he thought it would take four days to get the 16th and 9th Armies ashore. He was relatively confident, he said, that his ships and U-boats could maintain control of the seas between England and France from Brighton to Ramsgate for at least those four days. But again he emphatically insisted that this would be possible only if the Luftwaffe had control of the air.

Goering smiled. He now had the measure of the RAF and its much-vaunted fighters, he said, and the Luftwaffe was ready to strike. Hitler ordered him to begin on 10 August. The invasion was now scheduled for the first week of September to allow for the barges to be gathered. RAF bases would be bombed to destruction so that they could not be used and the British aircraft shot from the skies. Goering was confident he would achieve and maintain air supremacy over the key sea areas.

The heads of the army and navy were deeply relieved. They had never wanted to invade Britain in the first place, preferring to starve the island nation into surrender by a war of attrition. Now the responsibility for success or failure rested with the Luftwaffe.

The Luftwaffe was divided into five self-contained air fleets, or Luftflotten. Each had fighters, bombers, transport and reconnaissance aircraft as well as a planning staff, intelligence corps and supreme commander. Three of the Luftflotten were facing Britain: Luftflotte 2, Luftflotte 3 and Luftflotte 5. Luftflotten 1 and 4 were elsewhere in the Reich. This organisation was designed for co-operation with the army, enabling flexible tactical use of aircraft to support ground attacks. It was not so well designed for a large-scale aerial campaign, when the different Luftflotten should have co-operated with each other rather than carry out their own independent tactical strikes. Nevertheless, Goering was confident that his central command structure in Berlin would maintain the necessary overall control and guidance.

Luftflotte 2 was commanded by Field Marshal Albert Kesselring and was stationed in Belgium, Holland and northeastern France. Luftflotte 3, under Field Marshal Hugo Sperrle, was spread across northern France from Boulogne to Cherbourg. These squadrons were mostly based on military airfields that had been captured intact. Luftflotte 5 was located in Norway and Denmark.

Altogether the Germans had 998 normal bombers and 316 dive-bombers facing Britain, plus 227 Messerschmitt Me 110 and 702 Messerschmitt Bf 109 fighters. A key limiting factor was already emerging. The Bf 109 was the German's most effective fighter, but it had the shortest range. From bases in France it could only just reach London before needing to turn back. When engaged in fuel-hungry combat its range was even shorter. This meant it could escort bombers to the all-important target areas across southeastern Britain, but did not allow for much combat time once there.

The RAF, meanwhile, was also preparing for battle. On 24 July 1940 Fighter Command found that it had 996 fighter aircraft, of which about 660 were ready for instant action. Some of the others were undergoing routine maintenance or being refitted, but the most important limiting factor was the number of pilots. There were always some pilots off sick or injured, while a number had been lost in France and it was taking time to train the replacements.

It was that training which was proving to be controversial and the cause of difficulties. The new pilots were being trained according to the pre-war Fighter Command 'Directives for Fighter Command Attacks', the so-called 'Fighter Book'. This had been drawn up in the days of the later biplane fighters and when it was expected that German bombers would be arriving from the east unescorted by fighters. As the fighter pilots were finding, things were now very different in practice.

The Fighter Book assumed that most operations would be carried out by a squadron of twelve fighters. Each squadron was divided into two flights of six aircraft and each flight into two sections of three. Each section was to fly in what was termed the Vic formation, the more senior pilot flying in front of and slightly below the other two. When flying as a flight formation, the two sections would form up so that the section of the flight leader was in front of and to one side of the other. When flying as a squadron, the flight led by the squadron commander would be in front.

It was assumed that the enemy bombers would follow the same tactics as those used by RAF Bomber Command. This entailed the bombers flying in a rigid box-like formation so that the defensive guns of each aircraft protected those around it. There were three approved attack methods. In the first, each section of the squadron formed up in line astern and attacked the bomber formation in turn from astern. By the time the final section had completed its attack, the first would have reformed and be ready to attack again. The second style of attack had each section attacking as a Vic of three aircraft, the succeeding sections coming in from alternate flanks of the bomber formation. The third approved method had a flight formed of two Vics side by side attacking from behind the bombers.

These tactics were good for the conditions under which they had been devised, that is for relatively slow biplanes to attack bombers in a rigid formation. But war flying in 1940 was very different. German bombers tended to fly in slightly looser formations and were usually escorted by fighters. Each of the standard attacks authorised by Fighter Command

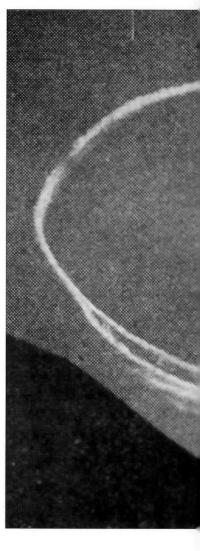

A squadron of Spitfires flies in close formation in the officially approved 4 Vic formation. By the time this photo was taken in August 1940 most squadrons had abandoned this grouping when entering combat.

called for the attacking squadron to spend some time adopting the correct formation. And during this time the escorting Messerschmitt fighters were diving down to attack.

Nor was this the only problem. The Vic formation meant that British fighters operated in units of three. Moreover, the emphasis on close formation had been fine for slow biplanes but called for constant concentration in the faster Hurricanes and Spitfires. This meant that the two wingmen spent

The twisting vapour trails left by fighter aircraft engaged in a dogfight high above England. Such trails became a common sight as the Battle of Britain reached its height.

nearly all their time concentrating on staying in position without colliding with the leader instead of scanning the skies for enemy aircraft.

The German fighters, by contrast, adopted the so-called 'finger four' formation. This was made up of four fighters flying in a looser formation with larger gaps between the aircraft. The first three fighters were in a loose line abreast, while the fourth flew some distance behind them, weaving slightly from side to side. The task of this 'weaver' was to keep a constant lookout behind the formation for enemy aircraft and his continual turning allowed him to scan the skies without there being a blind spot behind the aircraft. The 'finger four' gave the Germans an almost automatic advantage in numbers, 4:3, but was also much more suited to the high-speed fighters now in operation.

The air fighting over Dunkirk, and over the Channel since, had revealed

Three Hurricanes are refuelled from a truck during the hectic fighting of the Battle of Britain. The pilots in flying dress stand nearby awaiting the call to return to combat.

to British fighter pilots the weaknesses of their official tactics. By the end of July most squadrons had abandoned the Vic formation, but kept the division of a squadron into two flights. Fighters now often flew in pairs and kept station further apart than previously. There was similarly no longer a rigid insistence on flying in groups of twelve or six. As many pairs as were ready would take off for action when called for. Most pilots were now having their guns and sights altered so that the eight machine guns converged about 200 yards in front of the aircraft instead of the regulation 400. They had found that shooting from up close was much more effective.

The problem was that the training units were still instructing new pilots in the old system. When a pilot joined a squadron it took several days to retrain him in whatever tactics the squadron had adopted, and an experienced pilot had to be taken out of the fighting to do the retraining.

The first of the really busy days came to Tangmere's men on 8 August 1940. The Hurricanes of No 145 Squadron, led by Squadron Leader Peel were flying a standing patrol over a convoy off the Isle of Wight at around 16,000 ft. At 9 am Peel was alerted by radio to a radar plot showing enemy aircraft approaching from the southwest. Peel studied that sector of the sky and soon saw at a range of about ten miles a force of 36 Stukas approaching at a height of 6,000 ft. Above them was an escort of Messerschmitt fighters at around 12,000 ft. They showed no sign of having seen the Hurricanes.

When the German aircraft drew close enough, Peel put his nose down and led No 145 in a classic diving attack out of the sun. Surprise was total, and six Stukas were shot down before the Germans reacted. Then the Bf 109s came down to drive off the Hurricanes. There was a tangled dogfight, in which one Messerschmitt crashed into the sea.

Flight Lieutenant Boyd (right) shows a fellow pilot the hole (arrowed) in his flying helmet caused by a German bullet. It was perhaps the narrowest escape of any pilot flying out of Sussex during the war.

Flight Lieutenant Boyd, who was one of the No 145 pilots, was pulling up from firing at a Bf 109 when there was a sudden splintering crash as the perspex canopy shattered. Boyd's flying helmet was torn from his head and his flying goggles spun off and out of the broken canopy. A German bullet had ripped off the helmet and left a neat hole in it, but had amazingly missed his head.

As Peel re-formed No 145 Squadron after the clash he saw that one Hurricane was missing and assumed it had been shot down. In fact, the aircraft's engine had stopped inexplicably just as the pilot had started his initial dive alongside Peel. Going down without an engine, the pilot decided to stay in his aircraft until No 145 were through the German formation, then to bale out and take to his dinghy. As he dived through the Stukas, the pilot opened fire and was gratified to see a Stuka begin to emit smoke and flames from its engine.

The pilot then opened his canopy and pulled out his dinghy, at which point the Hurricane engine spluttered back into life as suddenly as it had died. Hurriedly regaining his seat, the pilot began to climb for height only for the engine to cut out again. This time he was close to shore and decided to glide his Hurricane in to land in a field. He then hopped out and walked back to the mess at Tangmere, to the surprise and delight of his comrades.

Back at Tangmere, No 145 Squadron was scrambled just before noon. The ten aircraft fit to fly took off and climbed for height as they made for Beachy Head, where radar had picked up incoming aircraft. Peel and his men had got to 20,000 ft by the time they arrived, but the Messerschmitt Me 110s were at 33,000 ft and quickly formed a defensive circle. Peel and his Hurricanes began the slow business of climbing up to their operational ceiling. As they reached about 28,000 ft, the Germans suddenly broke up their formation and dived for France.

Not for nothing had Goering had his aircraft probing British defences. His intelligence staff had built up a reasonably accurate picture of how effective the radar system was and how quickly Fighter Command could react. They also knew from captured RAF fighters left behind in France the capabilities of the aircraft they were facing. The apparent raid over Beachy Head had been a clever ruse. The Messerschmitts had drawn out No 145 Squadron, forcing them to burn up fuel climbing for height before suddenly fleeing.

At that precise moment, radar picked up a new formation of Stukas heading for the convoy off the Isle of Wight. No 145 was in no position to intervene, being some miles away and short of fuel. It had been a well-

planned operation by the Luftwaffe. Fortunately for the convoy, however, six Spitfires from No 609 Squadron in 10 Group were on a regular patrol and were able to race to the scene. As soon as they saw the approaching Spitfires, the Stuka pilots jettisoned their bombs and called off the attack. Even so, it was a grim indication of what the Luftwaffe could do.

Meanwhile Boyd's canopy had been repaired and, in company with another

A pair of Junkers Ju 87 Stuka divebombers roar low over an RAF fighter base in August 1940. The Stuka would soon be removed from such raids, as it proved to be vulnerable to RAF fighters.

pilot of No 145 Squadron, he had taken off to head for the convoy. They did not reach it before they came across six Messerschmitt Me 110 fighters and attacked them. Boyd and his partner shot down a German each on the first pass, then swooped around to return. Boyd misjudged his turn and put his Hurricane's nose up so steeply that it stalled. It was as well for him that it did, for as the aircraft fell off a Me 110 that Boyd had not seen flashed past him. Recovering control, Boyd gave chase. He caught the Me 110 over the Isle of Wight and, dodging bullets from the German's rear gun, shot it down.

It had been a busy day for No 145 Squadron, but it was not over yet. At 4 pm Peel, Boyd and No 145 Squadron were scrambled again, and once more the convoy was the German target. By this time the ships were off Swanage. As Peel approached he could see smoke and flames drifting up from the convoy and bomb splashes in the water, but no German aircraft could be seen. Unknown to Peel, this was the largest of the three attacks on the convoy, being made by 100 Stukas escorted by 50 Bf 109s. Four ships were to be sunk in this assault.

Peel began to circle his squadron as he peered down into the smoke. Suddenly the Bf 109s broke out of the smoke, zooming up towards the Hurricanes with their machine guns and cannon chattering. Peel himself got on the tail of one Messerschmitt, pouring a long burst into it. The German pilot threw back the canopy and clambered out. He waved briefly at Peel, then jumped. His parachute opened and he drifted down to land in the sea. Ironically, he was then picked up by one of the convoy ships his formation had moments earlier been trying to sink.

While the Messerschmitts kept the Hurricanes of No 145 Squadron busy in a dogfight, the Stukas headed for France. By the time the British pilots were free to give chase, the Stukas were out of range. For the third time, No 145 Squadron flew home to Tangmere and this time they were not called out again. At least, not that day.

Bad weather and delays in drawing up a properly phased plan of attack meant that the German offensive did not start until 13 August 1940, dubbed *Adlertag*, or Eagle Day, by Goering. The Germans flew 1,485 sorties that day, building to 1,786 two days later. The attacks pummelled British radar stations and RAF airfields.

Tangmere was hit by Stukas on 15 August; then again, harder, the next day. The officers' mess, storeroom, all the hangars, the hospital, the engineering workshops and several other buildings were destroyed. More than a dozen aircraft were destroyed on the ground and others lost in aerial combats.

One of the aircraft that managed to get off during the raid was piloted

---

Squadron Leader Peel commanded No 145 Squadron at Tangmere throughout the early stages of the Battle of Britain.

by Flying Officer Gordon Cleaver. Cleaver already had six confirmed kills to his credit, five of them shot down during the hectic month of May, in France. Now he gallantly raced over the airfield as bombs burst around his aircraft and, along with two others, got into the air. Not bothering with the usual tactical niceties of trying to gain height, Cleaver hurled himself at the nearest German aircraft, firing bullets from his eight machine guns. The German aircraft bucked sharply, then dived into the ground at high speed.

Cleaver then turned to a second German aircraft, but was caught in a hail of bullets from a swooping Messerschmitt. A splinter caught him in the right eye and cut across his nose. Blood spurted out, almost blinding Cleaver. Hurriedly he put his Hurricane down into a field and applied an emergency dressing to his wound. He had been in the air less than three minutes.

German reports had Tangmere marked as having been put out of action. Although badly damaged, the airfield was not completely knocked out and continued to put up its fighters. It was bombed again on 30 August and again badly damaged. Westhampnett, by now being used as a satellite airfield for Tangmere, was also heavily bombed as were Ford, Thorney Island and Shoreham, though these were not yet Fighter Command bases.

By mid-month one of the Hurricane pilots of No 43 Squadron at Tangmere, Sergeant Herbert Hallowes had achieved the figure of 20 enemy aircraft confirmed shot down, most of them over France. No 43 Squadron was sent up to intercept an incoming raid and Hallowes joined the attack as the squadron dived down out of the sun. He got behind a Junkers Ju 88, but, as he was about to fire, his own aircraft was hit by a spray of machine-gun bullets from the enemy bomber. The Hurricane's engine seized up and began to emit a stream of oil.

Realising that the fighter was doomed, Hallowes threw back the canopy and began to climb out. He got as far as having his right leg on the wing root when a terrific drumming announced the arrival of machine-gun bullets. Desperately looking around, Hallowes saw a Messerschmitt Bf 109 diving at him from behind, the orange flicker of machine guns firing from its wings.

Leaping back into the cockpit of his flaming Hurricane, Hallowes jinked sideways to evade the bullets, then hauled on the joystick to bring the nose of the Hurricane up and round as the Messerschmitt flashed past. Pushing the firing button, Hallowes sent a stream of bullets into the German aircraft. He then baled out properly and soon had the satisfaction of seeing the pilot from the Messerschmitt floating down alongside him to the Sussex fields.

Groundcrew rearm a Spitfire in August 1940. The thin elliptical wing of the Spitfire made this job a fiddly operation for the men.

Hallowes returned to his squadron, while the German was hauled off to a prisoner of war camp for the duration.

Hallowes' squadron commander considered the incident worthy of the award of a DFM and accordingly sent off a recommendation to 11 Group headquarters. A few days later he was startled to get a phone call from Air Vice Marshal Sir Keith Park querying the details on the form. Was it true, Park demanded, that this was Hallowes' 21st victory in the air? When told that it was, Park rather forcibly expressed the opinion that he should have been told about Sergeant Hallowes before.

Two weeks later the news came through to Tangmere that Hallowes had been awarded the DFM for his general devotion to duty, fighting skills and

No 43 Squadron's Sergeant Herbert Hallowes achieved his 21st confirmed kill when flying out of Tangmere during the Battle of Britain.

high score of enemy aircraft destroyed. And that he had been awarded an immediate Bar to the DFM for his fight with the Bf 109.

A few days later the announcement of another DFM award came through, this time for a pilot of No 602 Squadron based at Westhampnett. 'Sergeant Basil Whall', the citation read, 'has shown grit and judgement to prove that he is a first rate fighting pilot.' Although the award was officially to recognise the seven German aircraft that he had shot down over Sussex, it may have been his exploits in Norway that counted as much.

Whall had then been flying Gladiators with No 267 Squadron, led by Squadron Leader John 'Baldy' Donaldson. The Gladiators were chosen because they had a standard conversion kit to replace the undercarriage with skis so that they could be flown off frozen lakes. The squadron was based on Lake Lesjeskogen, from where it provided air cover to the British troops at Narvik. Whall himself was able to claim two German aircraft shot down, plus a probable, but the biplane Gladiators were generally outclassed. A devastating air raid by the Luftwaffe smashed the ice and destroyed most of the aircraft. The squadron then moved to Aandalesnes, where the remaining Gladiators were destroyed in another raid.

The surviving aircrew and ground crew of No 267 were put on board HMS *Glorious* to be taken back to Britain. Unfortunately *Glorious* ran into the German pocket battleship *Scharnhorst* and was sunk. Whall was among the few to be picked up by British ships and taken home. His squadron commander, Donaldson, was less lucky. He was picked up by a German destroyer and was so rude about Hitler that he was thrown back into the sea to drown.

A group photo of No 602 Squadron at Westhampnett in 1940. The squadron arrived in August 1940 and was immediately thrown into the thick of the Battle of Britain.

Heinkel 111

Type:	Five-crew medium bomber
Engine:	2 x 1200 hp Junkers Jumo 211D-1
Wingspan:	74 ft 1 in
Length:	53 ft 9 in
Height:	13 ft 1 in
Weight:	Empty 17,000 lb
	Loaded 30,865 lb
Armament:	1 x 20 mm cannon nose, 1 x 13 mm machine gun in dorsal position, 7 x 7.9 mm machine guns in ventral, beam and nose positions.
Bomb load:	7165 lb
Max speed:	252 mph
Ceiling:	21,980 ft
Range:	1280 miles
Production:	7300

The figures given above are for the Heinkel 111H, of which over 6000 were built. There were eleven other models, one of them a naval torpedo bomber, but these were built in only small numbers. The 'H' was the sixth model in the series and the first to have the distinctive glazed nose. The 111 first entered service in 1936, the 'H' model arriving in 1939. It was the mainstay of the Luftwaffe's bombing arm and was classified as a heavy bomber when it first appeared, though it is now generally reckoned a medium bomber in comparison to the Allied four-engined giants. The Luftwaffe remained primarily dedicated to helping the army by bombing military targets behind the front lines, plus the occasional terror raid, such as those on Warsaw and Rotterdam, to bully an enemy government into early surrender. In such roles the Heinkel 111 was supreme.

Chapter 4

Invasion Alert

Towards the end of August 1940, Goering held another top level conference of Luftwaffe commanders. The senior officers pored over the combat reports, intelligence analyses and other documents before discussing how best to complete the destruction of RAF Fighter Command in southeastern England. The results of that conference proved to be disastrous for Britain and came very close to handing victory to the Luftwaffe in what was now being seen by both sides as the Battle of Britain.

The first fact acknowledged by the Luftwaffe high command was that their intelligence reports were faulty. The strength of Fighter Command in terms of modern fighters had been badly underestimated, so that no matter how many Hurricanes and Spitfires were shot down there were still plenty more coming up to replace them. In fact the intelligence reports had not been so far off the mark as the Germans supposed. They had estimated fairly accurately the strength of Fighter Command, but had got wrong the speed with which Britain could turn out new fighters.

Goering, as a highly experienced fighter pilot from the First World War, would have known that in the hectic swirl of war

An Observer Corps post in August 1940. Each post was protected by sandbags and was manned permanently by two men, linked to a regional headquarters by phone. The Observers were responsible for positive identification of enemy aircraft types and numbers as well as plotting their movements once they crossed the coast.

The Hurricane production line at Hawker's factory. The ability of the British aircraft industry to pour out replacement fighters amazed the Germans.

flying it was quite easy for fighter pilots to claim to have shot down more enemy aircraft than in fact they had. Even when being completely honest, a fighter pilot might claim as destroyed an enemy aircraft that was in fact badly damaged and managed to limp home. Or two pilots might claim the same victim, as they both fired at it as it went down. What was almost impossible to know was the ratio at which the overclaiming occurred. After the war, historians compared the records of both sides and found that the British had been overclaiming by about 1.7 to 1 (the ratio was later to rise) at this period, while the Germans overclaimed by about 2 to 1.

If the actual aircraft were not being destroyed as fast as hoped, neither

A wounded German pilot shot down in August 1940 is given first aid while awaiting the arrival of a military ambulance to take him off to captivity.

were the airfields. The efficiency of repair crews meant that the RAF could get fighter bases back into operation much faster than the Germans thought possible. After a heavy bombing raid the Luftwaffe marked an airbase as destroyed, and estimated it would take at least two weeks to get it working again. In fact most Fighter Command airfields were back in at least partial operation within a day or two.

It was also becoming clear that the German bombers were more vulnerable to the British fighters than had been expected. They needed heavier and closer fighter support than they had been receiving. This led to a row between the senior fighter commanders and the senior bomber commanders. The fighter men pointed out that if they were flying close escort to the bombers then they would not be able to range freely about the skies to get into a good position from which to attack British aircraft. The bomber men retorted that, if the fighters freewheeled around the sky, they left the bombers wide open to British attack.

After some heated discussion Goering sided with the bombers. It was decided to concentrate on destroying the air bases of Fighter Command in southeastern England. If British fighters could be shot down, all well and

This Bf 109 was shot down over Eastbourne during a combat watched by thousands of civilians in August. Those not engaged in urgent tasks flocked to the hill outside the town to see the downed German fighter.

good, but since the British seemed to have limitless supplies it appeared foolish to try to win by shooting them all down. Much better to deny them landing fields and maintenance facilities.

This led to a distinct change in tactics by the Luftwaffe. The new priority was to get bombers through to their targets. Earlier decoys, such as the high-flying Messerschmitt Me 110s that had misled No 145 Squadron over Beachy Head, were recognised as having been successful. They were now put into operation on a grand scale. Because radar could not distinguish between types of aircraft, the Luftwaffe brought in numbers of transport or training aircraft. These were sent to circle over northern France as if they were bombers getting into formation ready to cross the Channel. They would set off for England, then at the last minute turn back. The British fighters sent to intercept this 'raid' would then return to base to refuel, at which point the real bombers would head over the Channel. Over the weeks that followed the Luftwaffe and RAF played out a deadly game of bluff and counter bluff as formations of real or decoy aircraft roamed the skies seeking to mislead the other side into making a mistake.

To add to the confusion, the Luftwaffe bombers no longer flew straight to their target and back again, but followed dog-legged and wandering courses that kept the British guessing as to where they should send their fighters. Many Luftwaffe operations now began as one massed formation, but broke up into as many as six different raids once over the English coast. British fighters began to waste a lot of fuel by being in the wrong place, so when they did eventually meet the Germans they were often as short of fuel as were the Luftwaffe fighters.

Goering also ordered that fighter squadrons were to be removed from Luftflotten 3 and 5 to be concentrated in Luftflotte 2. Flying from their bases closest to Britain, this put the fighters in a better position to have enough fuel for meaningful periods of combat over Britain. And while some fighters were to fly close escort to the bombers, sometimes as close as 200 ft, others were to fly distant escort. This meant that while they had to stay within sight of the bombers, as the bomber men wanted, they were relatively free to choose their own position and so could seek to bounce British fighters, as the German fighter pilots wanted.

The new plan was put into operation on 24 August 1940. It was an immediate success. Losses of German bombers fell dramatically, while the numbers of British fighters shot down rose. Although it was fighter bases in the southeast that were the main targets, the Luftwaffe kept Dowding guessing as to the target of each raid by also bombing factories, dockyards and railway junctions. Lacking fighter cover, the bombers of Luftflotten 3 and 5 now concentrated on night raids – that on Liverpool on 28 August was the heaviest thus far.

On the British side, the change in Luftwaffe tactics had a dramatic effect. Tangmere was hit on 30 August 1940 and the popular Squadron Leader Badger badly injured – he later died of his wounds. He was awarded a DFC while in hospital in recognition of his bravery and dedication to duty, as his official citation reads: 'It is through his personal leadership that the squadron has achieved so many successes since the intensive air operations began. Squadron Leader Badger has displayed great courage and resolution.' Badger's colleague in so many combats, Flight Lieutenant Robert Boyd, was also awarded a DFC at this time and some months later would gain a Bar to the medal.

The airfield was able to operate as a landing field, but its repair and maintenance facilities were out of action for days. Elsewhere the damage was even worse. The Germans were no longer content to bomb an airfield only once; now they came back again and again. Biggin Hill was out of operation for a couple of days and Manston had to be abandoned completely.

A few days after the bombing raid, ground crew at Tangmere were alerted by radio to the fact that one of their pilots, Billy Fiske, was coming back with a damaged Hurricane and a wounded leg. The fire crews and ambulance were alerted and, as the Hurricane came into view trailing oily black smoke, they moved out on to the landing strip. The Hurricane came down heavily and slewed over the field with emergency vehicles in chase. When it came to a halt, the fire crew got there first and began to hose down the burning machine, allowing the ambulance men to clamber on to the wings and smash the perspex canopy with hammers.

As the pilot was being hauled out, a sinister black shape dived down from the skies with machine guns chattering. The Messerschmitt Bf 109 that had wounded Fiske had followed him to base and was now coming down to finish the job. Despite the hail of bullets and cannon shells, the ambulancemen stuck to their task and got Fiske out of the burning aircraft. Unfortunately Fiske was later to die of his wounds, making him the first American to die fighting for the Allied cause.

By 2 September 1940, Dowding was seriously considering abandoning all his bases in southeastern England, including Tangmere and Westhampnett in Sussex. His overall priority was to stop the Germans having air control over the Channel when they launched their invasion. Dowding thought that by pulling his men and aircraft out of the range of the Messerschmitt Bf 109s he could keep his force relatively intact. Then, when the German invasion fleet put to sea, the Fighter Command squadrons could be raced south to operate from temporary grass airfields for the two or three days necessary.

It was a desperate gamble in more ways than one. Not only would Fighter Command be reduced to being able to mount only one three-day campaign, it would also leave London and the South East wide open to Luftwaffe attack. Unprotected by Fighter Command, the towns and cities would be pummelled by German bombs as Warsaw and Rotterdam had been before. Casualties would be huge and evacuation the only remedy. Panic would be unavoidable. If this continued long enough, Dowding feared, it might itself be enough to force a surrender even without a German invasion – though the minds of the British public were so closed to the idea of surrender that this seems unlikely.

On 3 September 1940 Fighter Command moved its squadrons around, shifting those that had borne the brunt of the fighting to quieter areas, while less war-torn units replaced them. At Tangmere, No 601 Squadron was sent to Exeter to rest and was replaced by No 213, which left Exeter that same day. The new squadron brought to Tangmere a section leader who already had a fearsome reputation as a war pilot and would go on to become one of the RAF's greatest pilots.

The new arrival was Dennis David, who had acquired the nickname 'Hurricane' by arriving with his first unit, No 87 Squadron, on the same day in 1939 that they transferred from Gladiators to Hurricanes. No 87 Squadron had been one of the first four squadrons to be sent out to France in September 1939 and David and his fellow pilots flew long, boring patrols up and down the frontier over the winter months, seeing nothing and gaining experience only in navigation. But on his first patrol on 10 May 1940 David had found the skies seemingly filled with German aircraft. The campaign that would end at Dunkirk had begun.

'Hurricane' achieved his first combat victory later that day when he shot down a Dornier Do 17 bomber over the Maginot Line. Next day he shot down a second and on the third day a Heinkel He 111. By now the speed and scope of the German advance was clear, so No 87 was pulled back to one temporary airfield after another. At one point the only shelter out of the rain to be had was a pigsty, so David slept there. On 20 May 1940 David was shot down and although he was not badly injured he was evacuated back to England. Scorning RAF medical treatment, David made his way home. His mother gave him a hot meal, and he then slept for a solid 36 hours.

David returned to duty to find that he had been transferred to No 213 Squadron and awarded both the DFC and Bar. He stayed with No 213 at Tangmere until November 1940, by which time he had increased his score to 15 confirmed kills and five unconfirmed, plus a number of probables and damageds. He was then promoted to Wing Commander and sent to No 152 Squadron, a Spitfire unit at Warmwell in Dorset. From there he was sent to Burma in 1943, with the rank of Group Captain, to act as the Senior Air Staff Officer with the Anglo-Indian forces facing the Japanese.

'Hurricane' David remained in the RAF after the war, flying Vampire jet fighters, before turning to diplomacy. He was the Air Attaché in Budapest when the Hungarian Uprising of 1956 took place. David used his diplomatic contacts to smuggle some 400 Hungarians out of the country before the vengeful Soviets could execute them. The escape earned him the nickname of the 'Light Blue Pimpernel'. He left the RAF in 1967 to work in engineering. He was later much in demand as a speaker and became a Freeman of the City of London. He died in 2000.

As Dowding agonised over whether or not to abandon Sussex and Kent in early September 1940, Hitler was making his decision for him. On 24 August a stray Luftwaffe bomber had lost its way at night. Its navigator was looking for a distinctive bend in the River Medway

Nicknamed 'Hurricane', Dennis David was awarded the DFC, and then the Bar just a few days later, during hectic fighting in 1940. He served as a flight commander with No 213 Squadron out of Tangmere during the Battle of Britain.

that would identify his target, but had found a similarly shaped bend of the Thames and so dropped his bombs on London. Churchill immediately ordered RAF Bomber Command to drop some bombs on Berlin. Although the British raid was only light and the bombs hopelessly scattered, it shattered Hitler's promise that no enemy could touch the Reich.

Hitler was furious. He in turn ordered Goering to attack British cities. Goering protested that Luftflotten 3 and 5 were already attacking by night. But Hitler wanted more: a massed daylight attack on London. Goering scheduled the attack for 7 September.

Coincidentally, RAF reconnaissance flights reported on the morning of 7 September 1940 that the number of transport ships and troop barges

A formation of Hurricane Mk 1s flies over England. The Hurricane was sold to the air forces of Belgium and Yugoslavia in some numbers during 1939 and 1940.

assembled in Channel ports had reached the point where they could transport the German invasion army. Churchill ordered that all units be put on invasion alert. Leave was cancelled, auxiliary units called up and men turned out of their barracks to occupy forward positions and emplacements. The Navy prepared to steam south to attack the invasion fleet.

That afternoon Goering and Kesselring stood on the cliffs near Calais to watch a vast armada of aircraft streaming northward over their heads. Over 300 bombers in solid layers from 13,500 to 19,000 ft were escorted by massed ranks of fighters below them, on either side and up as high as 30,000 ft. The usual decoy measures had been undertaken and, together with the vast size of this single raid, ensured that Fighter Command was taken unawares.

The Germans got through unhindered, opened their bomb doors in perfect formation and rained down their load on the East End and central London. In all, 300 civilians were killed and 1,300 seriously wounded, plus an unknown number of minor injuries. Hundreds of houses, factories and warehouses were flattened and thousands more damaged.

The change of target and tactics convinced the British high command that the German invasion would take place within the next three days. In fact,

Hitler had already postponed it from 10 September to 24 September, due to the continued presence of RAF Fighter Command. On 17 September bad weather caused another postponement and on 12 October 1940 it was put off until the spring.

On the day Hitler postponed the invasion, the Luftwaffe decided to try a new tactic. No longer under enormous pressure to destroy Fighter Command by a set date, Goering decided to try an ambush on the afternoon of 17 September. Instead of the normal mix of bombers and fighter escort, the raid on Sussex that day consisted of fighters only. About 200 Messerschmitt Bf 109s came over at 25,000 ft, arranged in ten different formations timed to arrive at various intervals to catch the RAF fighters in different stages of flight and refuelling, and then to overwhelm them by numbers. In the end this raid was only a partial success. Dogfights did take place but the Luftwaffe had not timed the raids precisely enough, so the RAF pilots were able to hold their own.

One Tangmere pilot landed to report that two Bf 109s had been destroyed, but that he was not actually claiming either of them as a kill. He had been on the tail of one Messerschmitt and was trying to get close enough to open fire when a second Messerschmitt had come diving down, to collide with the first. Both German aircraft broke up immediately and fell to earth, neither pilot surviving.

The raid was, however, a startling success for the Luftwaffe in a quite different way. Allied intelligence had picked up reports by way of neutral countries, such as the Soviet Union and Japan, that Germany was about to introduce a new and revolutionary fighter: the Heinkel He 113.

The Heinkel He 113 could fly at a startling 394 mph, about 40 mph faster than the Spitfire. The figures had been achieved, according to Russian sources, by no less a personage than the great Luftwaffe pilot Ernst Udet over a 100 km course. It was armed with a 20 mm cannon in the nose and two heavy machine guns in the wings. British intelligence found confirmation of these reports when they spotted the new, lean fighter appearing in the background of photos taken by journalists from neutral countries such as Romania and Hungary visiting Luftwaffe bases in Germany. That this was, indeed, the rumoured Heinkel He 113 seemed to be confirmed when the Gestapo demanded that the journalists hand over the negatives of those photos. Hurriedly, the intelligence officers went to work and counted twelve different squadron markings in the photos.

A series of recognition drawings of the new fighter with its elegantly tapering wings was produced and circulated to RAF pilots. They were told to keep an eye open for the new 'wonder fighter'. It was during this series of combats on 17 September 1940 that the RAF pilots from Tangmere first reported encountering the Heinkel He 113. The RAF high command buzzed with the news that the Luftwaffe's wonder fighter had arrived, and many began to fear that the Spitfire was soon to be outclassed and swept from the skies. The question everyone asked was simple: how many of these terrible new weapons did the Germans have?

The rather surprising answer was that the Germans had only a few prototypes of the Heinkel He 113, and two of those were unfit to fly. The whole thing had been a triumph for Goebbels and the Nazi propaganda machine. Ernst Udet had, indeed, achieved his speed record in a Heinkel He 113 fighter as the Russians had reported. However, Heinkel soon found that putting the aircraft into mass production would involve making changes to the air frame that reduced this speed to much the same as that of the Messerschmitt Bf 109. The Luftwaffe preferred the fighter it knew and refused to buy the He 113.

Goebbels, however, saw the propaganda potential and acquired the few He 113 fighters for his own purposes. It was he who had got them painted with the markings of so many different squadrons and who had left them standing around during the visits by Romanian and Hungarian journalists. And it was Goebbels again who then sent the Gestapo agents to demand the photos back, but only after carefully leaving enough time to ensure that it would be too late to stop publication.

The Heinkel He113 continued to be reported by RAF pilots throughout the autumn of 1940 and spring of 1941. In fact, they were seeing Messerschmitt Bf 109s and misreporting them. Once Goebbels finished with the few He 113s that did exist they were sent back to Heinkel, who formed them into a private combat squadron for the defence of their factories. It was in the summer of 1942 that the RAF realised that the new wonder fighter was not appearing in combat in any great numbers, but it was only after the war that the truth came out and the British realised that they had been duped.

But if the He 113 was a mere chimera, the Messerschmitt fighters were real enough. After the forays of 17 September, they came back again on 19 September and regularly thereafter. Dowding was puzzled by the purpose of these fighter raids. Were they decoy raids? Were they designed to disrupt civilian life by causing the air raid sirens to be sounded?

One pilot of No 601 Squadron sent up from Tangmere to face a fighter-only raid had an adventurous time. His name was not given in the contemporary reports, though the fact that he was Australian was given due prominence. This unfortunate Spitfire pilot was climbing for height when the oxygen system suddenly exploded. The cockpit flooded with pure oxygen and small sparks caught fire in the rarefied atmosphere. The pilot dived out of formation and then baled out.

Unfortunately, as he pulled his ripcord to open the parachute, a Spitfire passed close by and the slipstream caused him to tumble. The parachute ripped and the lines tangled, leaving the pilot upside down with his legs caught in the lines. Desperately kicking and wriggling, the man eventually got himself the right way up when only 500 ft from the ground, but the torn parachute meant he was falling so fast that he hit the ground with a terrific thump in the middle of a muddy potato field. He blacked out.

When the pilot came to, he found himself covered in mud as his parachute had been dragging him around the field. He was surrounded by half a dozen land girls, one of whom swiftly held a pitchfork to his throat as he began to move. Scraping off enough mud to reveal his RAF insignia, the pilot found himself unable to stand due to having sprained both ankles. The girls put down their makeshift weapons, then suddenly grabbed them again as a Home Guard patrol surged into the field with bayonets fixed. Another debate followed as the Home Guard were convinced that the blazing wreckage they had seen crash down half a mile away had been a Messerschmitt. The pilot, they maintained, was a German in disguise. The hapless pilot was put under arrest, and then released when the Home Guard officer turned up and was convinced of his RAF identity.

By this point a fire engine had arrived to put out the flaming wreck that was all that remained of the crashed Spitfire. When the fire was out the pilot was offered a lift back to the fire station in Arundel, from where he could phone Tangmere to arrange transport back to base. The pilot agreed and was perched up on the fire engine. Off went the fire engine, rattling down the country lanes at speed to return to its station in case it was needed to deal with falling bombs – it not having been realised the raid was by fighters only. The driver proved to be too enthusiastic. As the fire engine took a corner it skidded and capsized into a ditch.

The RAF pilot was thrown clear of the crash, this time injuring a wrist. He finally got back to base with only one limb working properly, having failed entirely to meet the enemy.

Another Tangmere pilot, Pilot Officer W.H. Millington, had an even narrower escape. He was engaged in combat over western Kent and was on the tail of a Messerschmitt Bf 109 when his fighter suddenly lurched to one side. He had been hit by cannon fire from another Bf 109, which then flashed past him. The Hurricane's engine was running rough, so Millington broke off combat and turned west to return to Tangmere.

As he headed for base, the engine grew rougher and rougher, losing power in fits and starts, and so the fighter lost altitude. The plane was down to barely 1000 ft when flames began to lick around the engine cowling. It was time to bale out. Throwing back the canopy, Millington was about to clamber from the cockpit, when he happened to glance ahead. There in full view was a small village, complete with church and school.

Dropping back into his seat, Millington grabbed the joystick and pushed forward to nose down towards a field. As the fighter increased in speed the flames grew brighter and longer as they licked back over the engine towards the cockpit. At the last moment he pulled the nose up, to pancake heavily into a field of turnips. The flaming Hurricane careered over the field until it came to rest. Millington now wasted no time scrambling out and running from the wreckage in his heavy flying boots. He had got only yards away when the fuel tanks exploded with a terrific blast that knocked Millington flat and badly burned the back of his flying suit and helmet.

In hospital a few days later, Millington felt well enough to deal with the inevitable paperwork. At the end of his combat report, completed to explain the loss of the Hurricane, he wrote: 'I considered it unwise to bale out, as my machine would probably have crashed into a village.' When he read this the squadron commander remarked, 'Observing the narrowness of his own escape, many pilots might have considered it unwise not to bale out.'

In fact, Goering was sending over his fighters simply so that they could try to ambush British squadrons and inflict heavy casualties. If they were unable to get into a good position, the Germans had orders to return to base. When Dowding did realise the true purpose of these raids he reacted quickly. Fighter Command was told to ignore them unless the Germans showed signs of coming down to low level to strafe targets. Even the largest formations of fighters at high level could do no damage to Britain, and Dowding thought his pilots too valuable to lose them in pointless combats.

Time and again, the pilots of Tangmere and Westhampnett sat in enforced leisure while watching the vapour trails of German fighters high above them. They hated it.

Dornier Do 17

Type:	five-crew medium bomber
Engine:	2 x 1000 hp Bramo Fafnir 323P
Wingspan:	59 ft
Length:	51 ft 9 in
Height:	14 ft 11 in
Weight:	Empty 13,145 lb
	Loaded 18,937 lb
Armament:	6 x 7.9 mm machine guns in various positions
Bombload:	2205 lb
Max speed:	263 mph
Ceiling:	26,740 ft
Range:	720 miles
Production:	1200

A pre-war photo of a Dornier Do 17P. Over 1200 Do 17s of various models were built between 1937 and 1941. Nicknamed the 'Flying Pencil', due to its slender fuselage, the Do 17 formed a major part of the Luftwaffe's bombing strength during the Battle of Britain.

Dornier's Do 17 range of bombers began in 1934 when Lufthansa rejected a Dornier design for a fast mail plane. By late 1935 Dornier had converted the prototype to a bomber with an internal bomb bay, machine gun mountings and a glazed nose. This entered Luftwaffe service in 1938 as the Do 17M, a bomber, and the Do 17P, a long range reconnaissance scout. It quickly acquired the nickname 'Flying Pencil', due to its thin fuselage. Experience in the Spanish Civil War highlighted problems with the bomber version, which by 1938 was replaced by the Do 17Z, to which the figures given here apply. This had a much enlarged front section of fuselage to house extra guns and other equipment. An export version was produced for Germany's allies, such as Hungary, but by 1942 the Luftwaffe was phasing the Do 17 out of front line service.

Messerschmitt Bf 109

Type:	Single-seat fighter
Engine:	1175 hp Daimler Benz DB601Aa
Wingspan:	32 ft 4 in
Length:	28 ft
Height:	8 ft 2 in
Weight:	Empty 4189 lb
	Loaded 5875 lb
Armament:	2 x 20 mm cannon plus 2 x 7.9 mm machine guns
Max speed:	348 mph
Ceiling:	34,450 ft
Range:	410 miles
Production:	35,000

When it joined the Luftwaffe as an operational fighter in the spring of 1937, the Messerschmitt Bf 109 was far and away the best fighter in the world. It was fast and nimble in combat, while its armament packed a mighty punch. The figures given here are for the 'E' model, which entered service in 1938 and was the dominant model during the Battle of Britain. The earlier models 'B', 'C' and 'D' had been powered by less powerful engines and by 1940 were used only for training. The 109 was produced in a further ten models with different engines and armament, there even being a ground-attack model equipped with bombs. By 1943 the 109 was increasingly being outclassed by more modern fighters, but it remained in production, as it was still a reliable workhorse for the Luftwaffe.

A Luftwaffe publicity photo of October 1939 shows a Messerschmitt Bf 109E ready to take off for a patrol along the French border. With two machine guns and two cannon, the Bf 109 was better armed than its French opponents.

Chapter 5

Messerschmitt Month

Once the invasion of Britain had been postponed to the spring of 1941 – and effectively cancelled – the nature of the air war over Britain changed dramatically. And not for the better so far as Fighter Command was concerned.

No longer having the need to crush Fighter Command to allow for an invasion by sea, the Luftwaffe was faced with a long campaign. There were effectively two options open to Goering and his air force. The first was to bomb Britain's industrial cities. This would slowly degrade the country's ability to wage war by destroying the armaments industries, halting fuel supplies and generally disrupting economic life to the point where Britain simply could not afford to pay the financial bills of war. The second was to act in concert with the German navy to starve Britain into surrender. While the U-boats and pocket battleships attacked convoys at sea, the Luftwaffe would pummel the docks and harbours where the convoys were to anchor. Given time, Britain would run out of food.

Whichever strategy was followed, there was a fair chance of success. Given a year, or maybe two, Britain would be brought to her knees and forced to come to some sort of peace deal with Germany. In the event, Goering and his senior commanders opted for a strategy blending the two ideas, though favouring the former, with some novel tactical and strategic ideas thrown in for good measure.

An RAF pilot makes a speech at a parachute factory in the Midlands. Tours around factories were much appreciated by the workers, who got to hear first hand how their products were being put to good use, and allowed the RAF to give aircrew a rest from the stress of combat.

However, the Luftwaffe's new direction depended for its success on having large numbers of new aircraft – just as the navy would need large numbers of U-boats and surface raiders. That in turn would mean the German armaments industry focusing efforts and raw materials on aircraft and naval construction. And the armed forces would have to begin training new recruits in the skills needed for air and sea warfare. That was never going to happen.

Unknown to anyone in the Luftwaffe or navy, except just possibly Goering himself, Hitler had lost interest in Britain when the invasion was called off. He was not interested in a long, grinding campaign of attrition even if it

The central control room of the Observer Corps. The staff at the bottom received reports from Observer Corps outposts and marked the position of all enemy aircraft on the table map. The staff on the balcony above reported those movements to Fighter Command HQ.

promised the near certainty of eventual victory. All of Hitler's successes, both in pre-war politics and in wartime conflict, had been won by swift, audacious blows that took the enemy by surprise. In any case, he had fought France and Britain only because they had intervened when he invaded Poland in September 1939.

Britain would, Hitler thought, have to be dealt with sometime. But he believed that the main reason Britain had refused his offers of peace was that Churchill was expecting help against Germany. Such help, Hitler reasoned, could come from only two places: the USA or the USSR. At this point the USA was showing no signs of joining the war, though it was clearly no friend of Germany's. That left the USSR, and Soviet Russia had long been a threat to Germany and a target of Hitler's hate.

While Hitler had been busy defeating France, the Soviets, under Josef Stalin, had occupied Lithuania, Latvia and Estonia as well as taking a slice of Finland. Hitler's belief that the move was the start of more widespread Soviet aggression seemed confirmed a few weeks later when Stalin demanded from Rumania the return of Rumanian-speaking Bessarabia, a one-time Tsarist possession that had joined Rumania during the First World War. Stalin gave Rumania only 24 hours to agree, or he would invade. Rumania handed over Bessarabia rather than risk war, and turned to Germany for help. Hitler was deeply concerned, for Germany's war machine depended entirely on Rumanian oil, and Stalin's bomber aircraft were now within range of the Rumanian oilfields.

For all these reasons, Hitler had by the end of September 1940 decided that Germany needed to launch a pre-emptive strike against Russia. It would take many months for plans to be drawn up, timetables to be agreed and the final decision to be taken – though taken it eventually was. What was important for Fighter Command about this train of events was that Hitler insisted that the focus of Germany's war industries and recruitment should remain on the army. If anything, the flow of men and resources to the Luftwaffe was reduced. Only aircraft that would support the army were to be built in any numbers. The mighty Heinkel He 177 Greif with its 14,000 lb bombload – similar to that of the RAF's Lancaster – was first delayed, then ordered only in fairly small numbers. The even more impressive He 277 was cancelled. The long-range maritime bomber, the Focke-Wulf Fw 200 Condor, fared even worse in terms of production.

Although ignorant of the reasons why they were not being given the aircraft and manpower that they demanded, the Luftwaffe commanders

were only too aware of the shortages. They drew up their plans for the campaign against Britain accordingly.

The first move was made in mid-September 1940. The Messerschmitt 110 had proved to be something of a disappointment. It had been designed as a long-range fighter to protect bombers on missions beyond the range of the Messerschmitt Bf 109. In the event, such missions had not proved necessary, due to the sudden collapse of France. In any case, the Me 110 had been outclassed in combat by the Spitfire and Hurricane. Despite the

A group of Hurricane pilots on an airfield, probably Tangmere, in September 1940.

impressive hitting power of its two cannon and four machine guns, the Me 110 was neither fast nor agile enough to match the RAF's single-seat fighters.

The Me 110 was, however, able to fly higher and faster than any bomber and its range was greater than that of the Bf 109. Its use in decoy raids during the Battle of Britain had shown that it stood a good chance of out-running British fighters if they were seen in time. Ever since it had been designed, Messerschmitt had had a conversion kit to turn the long-range fighter into a light bomber by the addition of under-wing bomb-racks. Now the bulk of the Me 110s were withdrawn from combat to be converted. By early in October, 250 converted fighter-bombers were ready for action.

These fighter-bombers proved to be a real problem for Fighter Command. Used against targets near the coast, they could fly in, bomb and get out again before the RAF had time to respond. Used in small groups, or even singly, they could penetrate quite a long way inland by flying at low level to deliver surprise assaults on all manner of targets. Carrying a maximum 2,000 lb of bombs, and considerably less on long raids, the Me 110 was never able to inflict serious damage on its targets.

These raids did, however, put a serious strain on Fighter Command's pilots and aircraft. Patrols had to be flown constantly from dawn until dusk, and other crews kept on standby for hour after hour. The overworked fighter aircraft began to break down with increased frequency, while pilots grew tired and often exhausted. So numerous did these raids become that Fighter Command pilots dubbed October 1940 'Messerschmitt month'.

The month opened on 5 October at 10 am when four waves of Messerschmitt Me 110 fighter-bombers crossed the Channel, escorted by Bf 109s. These came over Kent, one force reaching London. In the afternoon it was the turn of Sussex and Hampshire to be struck by the new tactic. Combats raged over Chichester and Southampton, with losses to both sides being about equal. The old cat and mouse game of decoy raids and dummy runs was continued by the Luftwaffe to try to catch Fighter Command out, while the British continued to misidentify Bf 109s as the elusive wonder fighter, the Heinkel He 113.

One Hurricane pilot from Tangmere got a nasty shock on 25 October. Aircraft were reported over Crawley when this pilot was already on patrol, so he was sent off to investigate while the rest of No 145 Squadron got airborne. The pilot got close enough to recognise the intruders as 50 Me 110s and reported the fact back by radio. He was ordered to head back toward Tangmere, rendezvous with his squadron en route and then join them in the attack on the fighter-bombers over Crawley.

As he flew southwest, the pilot saw a force of six fighters flying straight and level toward Crawley. Taking these to be a flight of No 145 Squadron, he dropped down and took up position behind them. A few minutes later the formation made a turn to the southeast, heading for Hastings. The pilot was puzzled by the move, but assumed the flight leader had seen something worth investigating. Suddenly the earphones of the hapless pilot burst into

A group of firemen crowd around a mobile tea canteen in London, September 1940. As German raids on the capital reached a climax the firemen had to eat and drink when they could.

life as his squadron comrades dived to attack the Me 110s over Crawley. Their excited warnings and reports, so typical of air combat, came flooding into the pilot's ears. And yet here he was flying serenely over Hastings.

And that was when he realised that he had joined a formation of Messerschmitt Bf 109s. In his sudden shock, the pilot pulled his aircraft's nose up. This must have caused one of the German pilots to look at him, for the enemy formation suddenly broke up as the pilots turned around to attack their unwelcome colleague.

*The famous church of St Clement Danes in London's Fleet Street goes up in flames.
Designed by Sir Christopher Wren to replace a medieval church destroyed in the
Great Fire of 1665, St Clement's was gutted by this fire started by incendiary bombs.
It was subsequently rebuilt and now serves as the home church of the RAF.*

The Hurricane pilot opened fire as a Bf 109 flew in front of him and saw pieces fly off the enemy aircraft. Then he barrel-rolled left and dived. A Bf 109 got on his tail, so he threw his aircraft around the sky until the enemy broke off. The hapless Hurricane pilot saw his assailant climbing away to rejoin the now re-formed Messerschmitt squadron, one of which was streaming glycol.

Turning for home, the Hurricane pilot was congratulating himself on a narrow escape when six more Bf 109s came diving down on him. The British

A fighter pilot makes his post-combat report to the squadron Intelligence Officer. The number of enemy aircraft encountered, how many damaged or shot down and their types were the prime consideration.

A Luftwaffe publicity photo from October 1940 shows Junkers Ju 88 bombers on their way to bomb England.

pilot pulled his nose up into a tight climbing turn to face the onslaught and opened fire. One of the Germans pulled up suddenly, usually a sign the pilot was hit, then flipped over and dived steeply. Once past the oncoming force of Germans, the Hurricane pilot himself went into a dive to gain speed as he headed towards the English coast. He saw no more of the enemy before landing back at Tangmere.

The following day an old Sussex hand, Squadron Leader Sir Archibald Hope, passed a significant milestone. When going up after yet another group of Messerschmitt raiders he flew his 100th combat mission since war had broken out a year and a month earlier.

In the middle of October 1940 a new development appeared. A force of Dornier Do 17 bombers was spotted by radar coming in over the Channel at 25,000 ft, a great height for this type of aircraft, escorted by Messerschmitt Bf 109 fighters. As the Tangmere fighters climbed up to intercept, the Dorniers turned away and dived back toward France. In accordance with standing orders not to rise to the bait of Bf 109 sweeps over England, the Hurricanes ignored the lone Bf 109s and returned to Tangmere.

But the Germans were in the new Bf 109E-4/N aircraft, with a 500 lb bomb tucked under the fuselage. Unmolested, the Messerschmitts flew on to attack their target, then hurried home. The trick was repeated several times in the following days before the RAF realised what was happening. But this new move was not the unqualified success that Goering had hoped for. As

A German Dornier bomber dives out of control towards the ground in September 1940.

The wreckage of a Heinkel He 111 bomber rests in the sea on a Sussex beach in the autumn of 1940.

the pilots of Fighter Command soon discovered, there was a problem with the new E-4/N version of the Bf 109.

The apparent fault was first reported by a pilot of No 501 Squadron, then based at Kenley, but formerly of Tangmere. His combat report explains how his squadron was sent up to face a force of these fighter-bomber conversions. He got on to the tail of one Bf 109E-4/N and opened fire: 'I gave it a three-second burst. No other action was necessary, as it disintegrated and fell from the sky in hundreds of pieces. I do not know if this was caused by a bomb or a petrol tank. It did not give me the impression of an explosion. It merely fell to pieces.' Two days later a pilot of No 249 made a similar report: 'The Messerschmitt disintegrated,' he wrote. 'Panels were falling off.' A pilot of No 501 reported next day that after firing a fleeting burst at maximum deflection at a Bf 109E-4/N, 'I saw the left wing fall off from the Messerschmitt, which dived out of control.'

When November came, bringing with it shorter days and worse weather, the daylight raids by Messerschmitt fighter-bombers slackened and then ceased. They would begin again in the spring, but never again in such numbers nor with such concentrated fury. Nor was the Bf 109E-4/N seen again. It had been replaced by the purpose-built Bf 109F-4B, with a more robust engine and redesigned wing assembly. Clearly there had been something wrong with the temporary conversion kit after all.

The Italian Air Force took part in the Battle of Britain with several bomber and fighter squadrons operating in coastal raids during September and October. This Fiat CR42 'Falco' was shot down in October 1940. Despite its antiquated appearance and performance, the CR42 had four machine guns and proved to be useful in second line duties.

Messerschmitt Me 110

Type: Two-seat long range fighter

Engine: 2 x 1100 hp Daimler-Benz DB601A

Wingspan: 53 ft 4 in

Length: 39 ft 8 in

Height: 11 ft 6 in

Weight: Empty 9920 lb
Loaded 15,300 lb

Armament: 2 x 20 mm cannon and 4 x 7.9 mm machine guns in nose plus 1 x 7.9 mm machine gun in rear cockpit

Max speed: 349 mph

Ceiling: 32,000 ft

Range: 565 miles

Production: 6050

A Messerschmitt Me 110D. This pre-war photograph shows the earliest operational version of the Me 110. Although armed with two cannon and five machine guns, the aircraft proved to lack the speed and agility needed for dogfighting. It was later produced in a variety of bomber, night fighter and ground attack versions.

Before the war began the Luftwaffe, unlike some other air forces, had worried that their bombers might not be able to fend off attacks by fighters. The need for an escort fighter with a similar range to the bombers was recognised, but the additional fuel tanks would make the resulting aircraft heavy. The answer, the Germans thought, was to provide twin engines and a heavy armament to give increased speed and hitting power to make up for a lack of nimbleness. The Me 110 entered service in July 1938 and by the time of the Battle of Britain was available in no less than seven variants, mostly concerned with armament or increased range. The figures given above are for the C5 model. After its lack of success against the Spitfire and Hurricane, the 110 was redesigned to be either a fast bomber or a night fighter in a further 20 variants. It remained in production to the end of 1944.

Chapter 6

Into the Night

Even while the pilots of Fighter Command were struggling to cope with the exhaustion of Messerschmitt month, an even greater threat was developing. This was the switch by the Luftwaffe's conventional bombers from daylight to night time assaults. The move had begun in a small way some weeks earlier when the Messerschmitt Bf 109s were concentrated in Luftflotte 2 to act as escort for the daylight bombing raids. The bombers of Luftflotten 3 and 5 had then begun flying at night to bomb British cities.

The night bombers had found both advantages and disadvantages to the new style of bombing. The most important advantage was that casualties fell immediately and dramatically. They had to risk the fire of anti-aircraft guns and the probing fingers of searchlights, but compared to running the gauntlet of Spitfire and Hurricane fighters this was minor. A second advantage was that they could afford to fly lower and slower than during daylight hours, and so could carry substantially heavier bombloads.

The drawback to bombing by night was navigation. Less than half bomber crews found their targets. The problem was not so bad when bombing coastal targets – such as ports or harbours – for it was relatively easy to distinguish between water and land. The very shape of the coast gave the crews a good idea of where they were. But over land the strict blackout enforced in Britain made it almost impossible to navigate with

A group of Hurricane pilots at rest in the officers' mess. The men are wearing 'night goggles', which enabled them to move around in lit rooms without spoiling their night vision. They would thus be able to take off immediately an enemy aircraft was located by radar to begin the difficult task of trying to spot it in the dark night sky.

any certainty. Thousands of bombs were wasted on empty fields instead of on factories and cities.

If navigation after dark was bad for the Luftwaffe, trying to track down enemy bombers was almost impossible for the men of Fighter Command. The night sky is a big place, and a bomber is a small thing to try to find, especially if it is painted black. During one night raid on London a total of over 700 German bombers attacked, while 41 fighters were airborne. Only two German bombers were even seen by British pilots, and only one shot down.

The best chance that a fighter pilot had of locating a bomber by night was either to wait for a night of full moon and hope to see the German aircraft by that pale light, or to hover around searchlight batteries and hope that they picked out a potential victim. One Tangmere Hurricane pilot was doing this over Southampton when a German bomber was caught by a searchlight at about 5,000 ft. The Hurricane pilot dived down, keeping his sights on the bomber and hoping that the searchlight crew would do their job and keep it securely fixed.

When 500 ft from the bomber, the British pilot moved his thumb to the firing button on his control stick. Before he could open fire the German suddenly exploded in a blinding flash of light. The wreckage of the bomber was found next day with its tail missing and scorch marks around the break. There is still no explanation of what happened.

Also successful, his colleagues thought almost supernaturally so, was Sergeant Andrew McDowell of No 602 Squadron, flying out of Westhampnett. In September 1940 this Spitfire squadron was given fairly basic training in night flying, then sent up to deal with nocturnal intruders. Most pilots failed even to sight an enemy, but McDowell was luckier – or perhaps better.

Several times McDowell managed to locate a German intruder and twice opened fire. Neither time was he able to confirm if the bomber had been destroyed or merely damaged, as the conflicts took place over the Channel. But when his finest moment came there could be no doubt at all. McDowell was up aloft when a small, loose formation of Germans was located heading for Westhampnett itself. McDowell raced to be over his airfield in time and was circling when the Germans arrived to bomb.

Down on the ground, the squadron personnel were taking cover, but enough of them were still in the open to see what happened next. Through the clear, moonlit sky the ominous shapes of the heavy bombers droned in at around 7,000 ft. Suddenly there was a stream of red tracer searing

across the sky, coming from the smaller black shape of a Spitfire attacking from head-on. The bomber erupted into flames and came crashing down into open country just outside the airfield perimeter. Given the high closing speed of a head-on attack this was a dangerous manoeuvre at night, but had been crowned by spectacular success. Already decorated with a DFC for his fighting in the Battle of Britain, McDowell was now awarded a Bar to the medal.

On the night of 14/15 November 1940, 449 German bombers undertook Operation Moonlight Sonata. Assisted by clear moonlight and new navigational aids, the Luftwaffe achieved a concentrated and accurate bombing of Coventry city centre, which was pulverised by incendiaries and high explosives. New phosphorous incendiaries could not be put out by sand, while parachute bombs exploded above ground to flatten a wider area than conventional bombs of the same power.

Something approaching a thousand people were killed in the city – the precise total has never been established – and destruction was widespread. The cathedral was gutted and the tram system was so badly damaged that

A Hurricane nightfighter awaits take-off. The only real adaptation to night fighting was to paint the aircraft black so that the German air gunners would find it harder to locate.

it never worked again. The Luftwaffe coined a new word, *coventrieren*, meaning to destroy utterly.

Such raids could not be allowed to continue. At the higher levels of the RAF, the debates and disagreements over how best to counter night bombers fed into older and more bitter disputes over how the fighter squadrons had been used before and during the Battle of Britain. The twists and turns of the arguments were complex, but the affair ended with Sir Hugh Dowding being removed as the head of Fighter Command. He had been due to move on to another appointment in any case, but the move left a bad feeling. He was not properly thanked by an honour for his work until some years later, and the manner in which he was given the news was tactless.

Even worse, from the point of view of Dowding's supporters, was the fact that he was replaced at the head of Fighter Command by one of his loudest and most vociferous critics: Air Marshal Sholto Douglas. And command of 11 Group, which included Sussex, was given to another critic, Air Vice Marshal Trafford Leigh-Mallory.

Douglas and Leigh-Mallory were fortunate that they arrived at a time when a revolutionary new aircraft was about to enter service. Development of the Beaufighter had begun under Dowding, but it was not until October 1940 that it entered service, and some weeks before it was flying in any numbers. The key to the success of the Beaufighter was that it was large enough to carry an airborne radar set and its operator as well as a pilot. Such twin-engined fighters – like the Messerschmitt Me 110 – had proved less than ideal in daylight combat, but at night it was another story. Vectored in by ground radar to an area where German aircraft were to be found, the Beaufighter crew then used the airborne radar to get within sight of the intruder. Only when a visual identification had been made would the pilot open fire; there were after all plenty of British aircraft aloft at night. The fearsome armament of the Beaufighter usually made short work of a target.

Among the first Beaufighters to enter service were those of No 219 Squadron that flew into Tangmere in October 1940. They were soon in action. The squadron was commanded by Squadron Leader James Little, who had taken command in May 1940, when they were flying Blenheim day fighters out of Catterick. The squadron had not had much luck in the north, but would do much better once they moved south.

The first German shot down using airborne radar, however, fell to the guns of No 604 Squadron on 19 November. Only three days later Tangmere's Beaufighters got their first success.

Flight Lieutenant Henry Goddard was up on a patrol over the south coast when radar picked up a lone German bomber coming in from the south at 20,000 ft. Goddard was sent after it, but the squally rain showers of that night caused problems. Twice his radar operator latched on to the intruder, and twice lost it again.

The third time he got a positive fix, the Beaufighter was in dense cloud. Goddard steered toward the invisible intruder, while his radar operator called out constant direction headings and ranges. As the Beaufighter emerged from the cloud, Goddard was startled to see the enemy, a Junkers

A Beaufighter Mk VI at rest. The unusual rounded nose of this example shows that it is fitted with the AI Mk VII air-to air-radar, introduced late in 1942.

Ju 88, barely 100 ft in front of him. He pushed the firing button, causing a stream of shot to pour out, then banked swiftly to avoid a collision. The radar operator glanced back to see the Junkers falling in flames.

A couple of weeks later, No 219's commander successfully intercepted and shot down a Dornier Do 17. Thereafter the RAF's night tally began to climb steadily. To explain this increasing success at night, the government put about the story that RAF Fighter Command pilots were on a diet of carrots after doctors had found that eating them improved night vision.

Because there were not yet enough Beaufighters to meet demand, Fighter Command brought its Blenheim Mk 1F aircraft out of the training and other secondary duties to which they had been consigned. Re-equipped with airborne radar, the Blenheims had a renewed lease of combat life. For a while they were the most numerous night fighters in the RAF and were not again taken out of frontline service until the Beaufighters replaced them in the early summer of 1941.

By this date Ford airfield had been taken over by Fighter Command, and No 23 Squadron was in residence with its radar-equipped Blenheims. Among the pilots was the ebullient Flying Officer Philip Ensor. Night after night, Ensor went up with No 23 Squadron to try to track down the German bombers. He located an enemy on three occasions, but failed to shoot down any one of them. He was, nevertheless, a popular officer whose consistent good humour did much to raise morale at Ford. It was largely for this invaluable contribution that he was awarded a DFM in February.

Another aircraft brought out of virtual retirement to fill the night fighter gap until the radar-equipped Beaufighter was available in sufficient numbers was the Boulton Paul Defiant. This fairly slow, heavy fighter was equipped with a four-gun turret behind the pilot, in which sat a gunner. The pre-war theory had been that these turret fighters would meet the large bomber formations as they came in over the North Sea and then fly alongside, shooting at them with their guns. Once France fell, however, German fighters could reach British skies and the anti-bomber Defiant was outclassed. But the Defiant was now brought back for night flying. It was the task of the gunner to scan the skies for an enemy while the pilot flew the aircraft.

A barrage balloon unit prepares to send a balloon aloft. These contraptions only rarely brought down a German aircraft, but they were highly effective at deterring low-flying bombing raids.

The Defiants were based in Kent and Surrey, being infrequent visitors to Tangmere and Ford. On 10 April 1941 some Defiants of No 264 Squadron were temporarily operating from Tangmere when German bombers were located by radar, coming in towards Beachy Head. Flight Lieutenant Eric Barwell, with Sergeant Martin as gunner, went up to intercept. They found a Heinkel He 111, but were spotted when about 300 yards away. Both Martin and the German rear gunner opened fire at the same moment. A brisk chase followed, which ended with the Heinkel suddenly diving vertically to the sea far below.

Despite the introduction of airborne radar, the German bombers were still getting through in large numbers. There were simply not enough radar-equipped Beaufighters to provide adequate defence. This was the time of the Blitz, when death and destruction rained down from the night skies.

Fortunately the defence of Britain from night bombing did not rely entirely on fighter aircraft. Also operating under the control of Fighter Command were the barrage balloons, searchlights and anti-aircraft batteries. Like Fighter Command, the ground-based defences had suffered from under-investment between the wars and even by the autumn of 1940 were not up to full strength.

The balloons were under the command of Air Vice Marshal O. T. Boyd, OBE, MC, AFC, who had his headquarters at RAF Stanmore, conveniently close to Bentley Priory. He divided his forces into groups, matching those of Fighter Command. According to the plans of the War Ministry, Boyd should have had over 2,000 balloons, but in fact had only 800.

Barrage balloons were large gas-filled balloons shaped rather like a torpedo with large fins at the rear. They were connected to the ground by a tough steel cable, by means of which they could be raised and lowered. From the balloons trailed a number of thinner wire cables that dangled down and blew about in the wind. In theory balloons were able to destroy any aircraft that flew into their cables – and several enemy bombers were in fact brought down in this way.

In practice, however, their main role was as a deterrent. Bomber pilots preferred not to go down lower than the balloons for fear of hitting the cables. When there was low cloud, the balloons could be positioned just beneath the cloud, thus blocking any bombing run. In clear weather the balloons were raised to their maximum height. This did not stop bombers flying higher than the balloons, of course, but did mean that they were bombing from high altitude. At this date bombsights did not allow for accurate bombing from much above 10,000 ft, so balloons could spoil the enemy's aim even if they could not stop him bombing entirely.

Unfortunately, destroying balloons was to become something of a sport for German fighter pilots engaged on sweeps over southern England. The balloons were filled with hydrogen, so if they were set on fire they would explode spectacularly. Some Luftwaffe pilots became very adept at balloon busting.

The Anti-Aircraft (AA) Command, widely known as 'ack-ack' during the war, had been formed in 1939 as part of the Territorial Army. However, it was soon obvious that close co-operation with fighter squadrons would be needed, so as soon as war broke out it was transferred to RAF Fighter Command. The officer in charge remained General Sir Frederick Pile and he preferred to keep his army organisation. The ack-ack was therefore organised into batteries grouped into divisions and remained so throughout the war.

Pile was supposed to have a strength of 2,232 heavy and 1,200 light guns, but in May 1940 he could count only 695 heavy and 253 light guns. Several of those guns were in France protecting RAF bases and were lost in the retreat to Dunkirk. Production was, however, proceeding quickly and by the time the main night-bombing offensive began, Britain had 1,195 heavy guns plus 585 light guns. Nevertheless, what Pile was still short of was trained gunners. In early 1941 an appeal to the Home Guard produced a large number of World War I artillery veterans, but they were available only part time and close to their homes.

Throughout the night bombing assault of 1940-41, the ack-ack depended largely on sound to locate bombers. Radar did not then operate over inland areas, so gunners were reduced to listening out for approaching raiders. As there was little point hoping to aim at individual bombers, the ack-ack aimed at putting up a 'roof' of exploding shells over a town or factory complex so that any bomber flying directly overhead was liable to be hit. Inevitably successes were few, but like the balloons they did serve to spoil the aim of the Germans.

Ack-ack guns achieved much greater success when accompanied by searchlights. If a German aircraft was illuminated by a searchlight, the gunners could actually aim at it, and so stood a much better chance of destroying the bomber. The Germans were, of course, well aware of this. Any bomber caught in a searchlight would fire its machine guns at the source of the light in the hope of either knocking it out or killing its crew.

A battery of heavy 4.5in anti-aircraft guns. Unlike the lighter 3.7in guns, these weapons required permanent concrete footings from which to fire. They were usually deployed around towns and cities.

A 3.7in anti-aircraft gun prepares for action. The gun crews trained for action in daylight hours and in the early months of the air war proved to be highly effective in this role.

117

A searchlight crew sweep the night skies for German bombers in the early months of 1941. Searchlight crews had the highest casualty rates of all the anti-aircraft units during the war.

As time passed, some German night fighters were sent over with bombers specifically to launch attacks on searchlights. The casualty rates among searchlight crews were high.

To ensure that the ack-ack did not inadvertently shoot down British night fighters, the country was carved up into Gun Defended Areas (GDA) and Fighter Defended Areas (FDA). Barrage balloons, searchlights and ack-ack guns were concentrated in GDAs, with orders to shoot at anything they could reach. The night fighters prowled in the FDAs, and had strict orders to avoid GDAs so as not to risk being shot down.

The anti-aircraft gun batteries each consisted of four heavy guns, or several lighter guns, and were positioned on hills or open fields from which they would have a clear field of fire to the area of sky along which enemy bombers were expected to fly when attacking a target. These sites were very often a long way from any village or town. One Londoner sent to man a base in Sussex set out one day to sample the local social life. He found a farmer trimming a hedge and asked, 'Where is the nearest town or pub, and when is the next bus?' The farmer eyed him quizzically and replied, 'About twelve miles, six miles and Wednesday,' then returned to his work.

Because of this isolation, each battery had to be entirely self-sufficient. At first the guns tended to be dispersed around the perimeter of the site, with control post, barracks and other buildings in the centre. War experience showed that this was not the best arrangement, as German bombers attacking the guns often hit the central area rather than the entrenched guns. One cook had the deeply disturbing experience on the night of 2 May 1940 of having an incendiary bomb crash through the roof of his wooden kitchen and land in a five gallon vat of soup. The soup put out the fire bomb, but the gunners went hungry.

As with so much about Fighter Command, the whole anti-aircraft gun system had been developed on the assumption that the enemy bombers would come by day. During the Battle of Britain, most raids were indeed during daylight hours. The guns did good work deterring attacks or driving them to a greater altitude, and a few German aircraft were brought down. But when the Luftwaffe switched to night attacks things became more difficult. At first gunners were given an estimated height by radar plot, then told to fire toward the sounds of engines.

As searchlights became more numerous the situation was eased somewhat. Then the increased number of guns allowed the gunners to put up a co-ordinated system of shots that was designed to fill each section of a box of air with an exploding shell. Any aircraft flying into that box would be hit, the theory went. At first the Germans learned to evade this system by changing their altitude over the target. Later short range radar was introduced that pinpointed the position of a raider in the dark sky, allowing gunfire to become more accurate.

In December 1941 women began to man searchlights and anti-aircraft guns. General Pile had launched the initiative, as he believed that women could do the work as well as men, who would then be freed up for other tasks. At first batteries were mixed affairs, with women undertaking the support and range-finding duties and the men working the guns. The mixed arrangements were expected to cause all sorts of problems and much work went into planning new washing and toilet facilities, but the most intransigent issue turned out to be the most unexpected: food. The women tended to want fresh fruit and salad, the men demanded meat and solid puddings. None of the kitchens was equipped to turn out two different meals at once, so one or other sex had to be disappointed. Once additional cookers and pans were introduced the problems were solved, but it took time. Meanwhile women-only crews had been taking over searchlight batteries and balloon barrages. By the end of 1942 women were in the majority.

The role of women in manning the air defences of Britain was celebrated at the time, but has rather gone unremarked since. But if it had not been for these gallant women risking sudden death at the hands of vengeful Luftwaffe machine-gunners, the men flying the nightfighters would have had no searchlights to help them, nor GDAs to take the pressure off them.

One of the first 'mixed' anti-aircraft batteries goes into action in 1941. The women man the direction finder in the foreground while men fire the gun in the background.

Bristol Beaufighter

Type:	Twin-seat night fighter
Engine:	2 x 1400 Bristol Hercules III
Wingspan:	57 ft 10 in
Length:	41 ft 4 in
Height:	15 ft 10 in
Weight:	Empty 14,069 lb Loaded 21,100 lb
Armament:	4 x 20 mm cannon in nose plus 6 x .303 machine guns in wings
Max speed:	323 mph
Ceiling:	28,900 ft
Range:	1170 miles
Production:	5584

The superb Beaufighter grew out of the equally impressive Beaufort, a long-range bomber developed for Coastal Command, that could carry a torpedo as an alternative to conventional bombs. It entered production late in 1939, with the first aircraft reaching Fighter Command in October 1940. The concept was to have a fighter large enough to carry an air-to-air radar set and a second crew member to operate it. The designers assumed that there would be time for only a short burst of fire at a target, hence the heavy armament. The Beaufighter was later modified to be an anti-shipping strike aircraft able to carry either rockets or a torpedo in addition to its cannon. The unusually quiet engines of this aircraft caused it to be nicknamed 'whispering death' by the Japanese.

A Bristol Beaufighter Mk 1, as shown in the first photograph of the aircraft to be released to the public. Although it gained fame as a night fighter, the Beaufighter went on to fill a range of roles.

Chapter 7

Back to France

As the long winter nights of 1940/41 began to shorten, Air Marshal Sholto Douglas began to lay his plans for the coming months. It was widely believed that Hitler had postponed the invasion of Britain until the spring of 1941. At some point, it was thought, a new Battle of Britain would break out as the Germans once again sought to achieve air supremacy over the English Channel and surrounding areas. Douglas began to lay his preparations to face the expected onslaught.

Meanwhile, the night bomber campaign continued. London was hit night after night for weeks on end, while other towns and cities received the attentions of the Luftwaffe less often. RAF night fighter squadrons were concentrated in the south and east to catch the bombers as they flew over the coast, both coming and going. A few squadrons were, however, stationed close to major cities such as Liverpool and Bristol to attack bombers as they closed in on these targets.

However, both Douglas and Leigh-Mallory were veterans of fighter squadrons in World War I, in what were known as scout squadrons. That war had ground on for years while being fought across a very static battleground around the trenches of the Western Front. When Douglas and Leigh-Mallory had been flying towards the end of the war it had been usual for British scouts to fly into the skies over the German rear areas to strafe ground targets, seek out German aircraft and generally make a

A Bristol Beaufighter Mk 1 flies over a snow-covered Britain in early 1941. The introduction of this aircraft in March 1941 revolutionised the RAF's night fighter effort.

nuisance of themselves. Now, they thought, it was time to do the same to the Germans in France, with the Channel taking the place of the static trenches.

The way had been shown as early as December 1940 when two pilots of No 66 Squadron had flow their Spitfires over the Channel to shoot up the Luftwaffe base at Le Touquet airfield. Douglas issued an order allowing any

Fighter Command was controlled from this room at RAF Bentley Priory. The table map plotted the movements of all aircraft, while the officers on the balcony above decided when to alert squadrons to intercept.

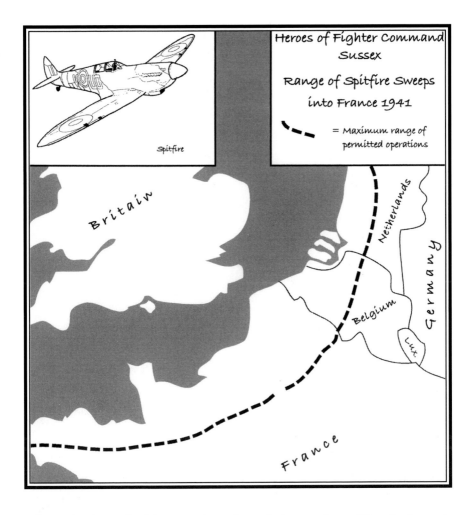

Heroes of Fighter Command
Sussex

Range of Spitfire Sweeps
into France 1941

= Maximum range of
permitted operations

Spitfire

Britain

Netherlands

Germany

Belgium

Lux.

France

pilots who fancied taking part in such a mission to do so. They had to ask permission of their Group HQ, giving details of intended targets and time of raid. Given that 11 Group was commanded by Leigh-Mallory, permission was usually given so long as there was plenty of cloud about in which the aircraft could seek shelter if they ran into heavy opposition. These missions became known as 'rhubarbs'.

More formal were other offensive missions, generally known as 'sweeps', being devised by Fighter Command. A 'rodeo' was essentially a rhubarb on a larger scale with two or more squadrons of fighters flying over to France to attack any ground targets that could be found, or to engage German

A squadron of Hurricane Mk II fighters in flight. The Mk II entered service in 1941 with an uprated engine and a much more effective armament of four 20 mm cannon. Not visible here are the two 500 lb bombs this version could carry under the wings. The Mk II carved out a career as a ground-attack aircraft during 1941 and 1942.

The pilots of an unnamed Hurricane squadron 'somewhere in England' show off to the press the Messerschmitt propeller blade on which they have kept a tally of the squadron's confirmed kills. The lower section is for action in France, the middle section action in England and the top – with only one kill mark – for night fighting.

Photographed 'somewhere in England' in July 1941, this Spitfire pilot has just returned from a 'rhubarb' mission over France. While groundcrew swarm over the aircraft to inspect it for damage and decide how much fuel and ammunition it needs, an intelligence officer (far right) talks to the pilot.

aircraft that were in the air. A 'Jim Crow' was a routine patrol along a set route over the English Channel to watch for movements by enemy aircraft or shipping.

A 'ramrod' was a bombing mission in which a small number of bombers flew over to France, in daylight and at low level, to bomb a specific target. RAF Bomber Command, like the Luftwaffe, had learned that massed daylight bomber raids were horribly vulnerable to fighters. They preferred to bomb at night, or with heavy fighter escort. Ramrods were, therefore, flown only within the operational range of Spitfires and Hurricanes operating from Britain.

'Circus' raids were similar to ramrods, but with the key difference that the bombing of the target was not the main objective. In fact, the targets of a circus were the fighter aircraft of the Luftwaffe. The bombers were there primarily to convince the Germans that it was a bombing raid. The British fighter escort was much larger than for a ramrod and had as its aim to ambush the Germans. Once the British fighters were engaged, the bombers

Two Spitfire squadrons set off for a circus operation over France. The second squadron is above and behind the first squadron to form an upper escort.

would very often return home.

While Fighter Command was putting these new offensive tactics into operation, it was also being reorganised. Leigh-Mallory had frequently criticised Dowding for using the squadron as the basic tactical unit. He had argued that fighters were much more effective if used in wings of three squadrons. Dowding had countered that in the hectic days of the Battle of Britain there was simply not enough time to get a wing organised, for by then the German bombers would have had time to drop their loads and head home. Now that Fighter Command was going on the offensive, Leigh-Mallory convinced Douglas to adopt the wing not just as a tactical unit but as an organisational structure.

All the day squadrons in Fighter Command were to be grouped into wings, each to be based at and take its name from a major station. Within each wing at least one squadron was equipped with Spitfires. Sussex was to be given just one wing, based at Tangmere, with nearby Ford and Westhampnett as subsidiary stations. This new Tangmere Wing was put under the command of one of the RAF's most famous aces: Douglas Bader.

Bader had been born in London, the son of a regular army officer who was to die of wounds received in the trenches of World War I. He was subsequently brought up by his mother's second husband, a Yorkshire vicar. In 1928 he joined the RAF, was posted to a fighter squadron flying Bulldog biplanes and soon proved to be a highly skilled pilot. In 1931 he was putting his Bulldog through some highly unofficial low level aerobatics when his wingtip hit the ground and he was piled up in a serious accident. He was rushed to hospital and his life saved only by the amputation of both legs, one above and one below the knee.

Bader made a dramatic recovery and by 1934 was able to fly with the aid of a pair of 'tin legs'. Nevertheless the RAF invalided him out and he took a job with an oil company and got married. In 1939 he rejoined as the outbreak of war made his skills and experience once again useful to the RAF. He retrained to fly Spitfires and by early 1940 was a Flying Officer on a fighter squadron in 12 Group.

Right from the start of his fighter career, Bader loudly espoused what he termed his Three Basic Rules:

- If you had the height, you controlled the battle.
- If you came out of the sun, the enemy could not see you.
- If you held your fire until you were very close, you seldom missed.

Douglas Bader (centre) and two fellow pilots of his Tangmere Wing inspect a piece of nose art on Bader's Spitfire. It shows a foot in a RAF flying boot delivering a hefty kick to Hitler's backside. It was painted by a member of the groundcrew who had been a signpainter in civilian life.

To this he often added a fourth, less formal rule:

Rules are for the guidance of wise men and the obedience of fools.

After a spell in Yorkshire, Bader returned to Essex at the height of the Battle of Britain. He now commanded No 242 Squadron, and strove to make it the most effective in the RAF. He also became convinced of the wing theory. Bader himself often waited until he had several squadrons together before going to attack German bomber formations, a move that proved controversial to say the least, but which stood him in good stead when Sholto Douglas became head of Fighter Command. Thus it was that he came to lead the Tangmere Wing on 18 March 1941.

Bader and his wing got off to a flying start, literally. On 19 March they went up to fly a Jim Crow patrol over the Channel. Two Messerschmitt Bf 109s managed to get behind the wing without being spotted and launched a high speed diving attack. One Spitfire was shot down, though the pilot managed to get out uninjured. The Spitfires gave chase, and Sergeant Payne of No 610 Squadron succeeded in catching up with and shooting down one of the German fighters.

Squadron Leader Douglas Bader. His exploits in the Battle of Britain had already made Bader a household name before he took command of the Tangmere Wing in early 1941.

On 10 April a Junkers Ju 88 came off the Channel at Bognor Regis, flying fast and low. It raced over Tangmere, dropping a full load of bombs that destroyed assorted buildings and killed five men before it disappeared back over the Channel as fast as it had come. A delayed action bomb was found outside the watch office, so the area was cordoned off until the bomb disposal teams arrived. Although severely depleted by the need to send aircraft to join the Russian campaign, the Luftwaffe had not given up the task of bombing Fighter Command airfields.

On the evening of 7 May 1941, a group of Tangmere Wing pilots sat up discussing tactics in the bar. Such a thing was not unusual, but on this occasion Flight Lieutenant Hugh Dundas loudly explained an idea of his. He suggested that if four Spitfires flew in line abreast, each about 60 yards from the next, they would be able to use their rear view mirrors to cover each other's blindspots. The concept was not, in fact, new. What was new was that this time Bader was listening. Next morning he strode into the officers' mess to announce that they were going to try the idea.

Up went Bader, Dundas and two other pilots. They adopted the four-abreast formation to fly up and down the Channel, close to the French coast. After half an hour, six Bf 109s were seen stalking the formation from behind. As Dundas had predicted, the Germans were quickly spotted. Bader decided to continue flying as if the Germans had not been seen to lure the Germans close enough so that they could, in turn, be caught off guard by a sudden about-face and attack performed by the Spitfires.

As the Bf 109s closed in, Bader gave the command for the Spitfires to break aside in pairs to sweep around and attack. With hindsight he gave the order too soon, allowing the Germans time to react. Nevertheless, one Bf 109 was shot down. Unfortunately, Dundas's Spitfire was badly damaged and only just managed to get as far as the English coast before he had to crashland into a field.

Bader judged the experiment to have been a success and at once insisted that his entire wing adopt what became known as the 'crossover four' as the basic fighter tactical formation. The idea spread through Fighter Command and many other squadrons followed suit.

A few days later, on 17 May 1941, Sergeant Morton of 145 Squadron was in the air with two new pilots, fresh out of training. He was about to begin a practical demonstration of approved dogfight moves when two fighters came into view heading for the Channel. Morton thought they looked like Bf 109s, but when he saw rounded wingtips concluded they must be Hurricanes, as the Bf 109 was easily recognisable by its square wingtips.

Then the two strangers flashed by, showing that they had yellow engine cowlings. Only German aircraft sported such markings. Shouting the warning 'Come on chaps, this is the real thing', Morton dived to give chase. To his amazement he was totally unable to catch up with the Bf 109s despite having the advantage of height. It later turned out that this was the first appearance of the new model of 109, the Bf 109F, which would prove to be superior to earlier models in terms of both speed and agility. It was perhaps as well that the two Bf 109s had been intent on getting home rather than staying to tackle Morton and his two pupils.

The sheer pressure experienced by the pilots of Fighter Command can be gauged by the operations records of the Tangmere Wing for June 1941:

4 June: Rhubarb to Le Havre in the morning followed by a rodeo to Le Touquet. No combats.

11 June: A rhubarb at 9 am and anther at 11 am. At 4 pm a rodeo set off for Cap Griz Nez, passing Le Touquet. No combats.

13 June: 7 am a rodeo to Calais. Four Bf 109s sighted, but no combat.

14 June: Rodeo at wing strength to Calais. No combat.

15 June: Rhubarb to Le Touquet. No combat.

17 June: Circus No 13 to Calais. Combat with Bf 109s took place, but no claims were made nor casualties reported.

18 June: Circus No 15 to Dunkirk. Two separate combats with Bf 109s resulted in one confirmed kill, two Spitfires shot down and one damaged.

19 June: Ramrod to Le Havre. Prolonged combat with a force of Bf 109s resulted in one claim of a damaged Bf 109, and no losses. Rhubarb to Gravelines resulted in no combats.

21 June: Circus No 17 to St Omer. Combats with Bf 109s resulted in three confirmed and three unconfirmed kills. Two Spitfires were shot down and two badly damaged, with one pilot being wounded. Two of the bombers were also lost.

22 June: Ramrod to St Omer. Three Bf 109s claimed as destroyed, though none confirmed.

23 June: At noon a rodeo to Le Touquet, no combat. At 7 pm a rodeo to Calais resulting in one Spitfire shot down and six damaged but no claims of damage to the enemy.

A Spitfire of No 616 Squadron parked on the ground at Tangmere in the summer of 1941.

24 June: Rodeo to Gravelines, no combats.

25 June: At noon, circus No 22 to Gravelines. Prolonged combats resulted in three Bf 109s destroyed and two damaged while one Spitfire was damaged. At 4 pm, circus No 23 to Le Touquet. Three Bf 109s were claimed as destroyed and four damaged. One Spitfire was badly damaged.

26 June: Circus No 24 to Gravelines. Three Bf 109s were claimed destroyed and two damaged. One Spitfire was shot down and a second damaged beyond repair.

27 June: At 1 pm a rodeo to Caen, no combats. At 8 pm a rodeo to Boulogne. One Bf 109 claimed as damaged in a short combat.

28 June: At 7 am circus No 26 to Dunkirk. One Bf 109 claimed as damaged.

30 June: Rodeo to St Omer. One Bf 109 claimed as damaged, one Spitfire damaged.

The Spitfire lost on 26 June was that of Flight Lieutenant Casson, who had to admit it was entirely his own fault. He had been so concerned with watching the skies that he had lost track of both time and distance. So when he turned north for England he was 50 miles further east than he thought. Unsurprisingly, he failed to find Tangmere and, after stooging around over Kent for some time, decided to land in a grassy meadow. Unfortunately for Casson he landed on what was not grass, but short wheat beneath which was the heavily rutted and soft soil of a ploughed field. The wheels snapped off as soon as they touched down, causing the Spitfire to skid on its belly before turning around 180 degrees. The tail then dug into the soft soil, flipping the aircraft into a backward somersault and breaking off the tail just behind the cockpit. Astonishingly, Casson was uninjured.

As can be appreciated, the Tangmere Wing was very busy with operational duties. These flights were on top of the usual training and test flights carried

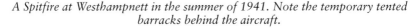

A Spitfire at Westhampnett in the summer of 1941. Note the temporary tented barracks behind the aircraft.

Ground crew rush to rearm a Hurricane at Tangmere in the summer of 1941. The constant offensive actions of that summer put a great strain on the mechanics and others on the ground.

out by any operational squadron, as well as the hours spent on aircraft recognition, tactical appreciation and other instruction. It is no wonder that for so many fighter pilots, tiredness was their main memory of that summer.

On 9 August 1941 the Tangmere Wing was sent out to make a sweep over the coast of northern France. Over Le Touquet, Bader and his wing became engaged in a dogfight with the Messerschmitt Bf 109s of German fighter squadron No 26. In the following battle, Bader's tail was shot off. Bader threw back his canopy and tried to bale out, but found that one of his false legs was trapped. He escaped only by breaking the straps that held the false leg in place.

There has since been much controversy over exactly how Bader was

A Luftwaffe publicity photo issued in the summer of 1941 shows a Bf 109 on the tail of a Spitfire over France. The original caption stressed the supposed superiority of the 109 in combat.

downed. He himself wrote home that he had collided with a Bf 109. However, the Germans knew that no Luftwaffe pilot had reported a collision and instead credited the feat to Feldwebel Meyer, who had reported shooting down a Spitfire. Recent research, however, has proved that Meyer had shot down a different Spitfire in a different place.

No 616 Squadron's Flight Lieutenant 'Buck' Casson, on the other hand, reported shooting down a Bf 109, the tail of which broke off at about the place and time that Bader was shot down. German records show that no Bf 109 was lost at that place. It seems likely that Bader was shot down by a Spitfire that mistook his aircraft for a German in the confused hurly burly of a dogfight. Presumably Bader invented the collision story to spare a fellow pilot's feelings.

Bader was by this time the most famous fighter pilot in Britain, with 22 confirmed kills in combat. When he was taken prisoner, he was met by Adolf Galland, the Luftwaffe's leading ace. Galland arranged for the RAF to be given safe conduct to drop a replacement leg for Bader, the resulting Operation Leg taking place on 19 August. Bader proved to be a major annoyance to the Germans and was sent to the notorious Colditz Castle to keep him both safe and out of the way. He remained there until the place was liberated by the American army in April 1945.

After the war Bader left the RAF to return to the oil business and forged a successful career with Shell. He devoted long hours to the cause of disabled people, for which he was knighted in 1976. Bader died in 1982 after a sudden, massive heart attack just days after speaking at a dinner to honour the 90th birthday of Sir Arthur Harris, head of RAF Bomber Command during most of the war. Soon after his death, a pub in Tangmere was renamed the Bader Arms.

Although the Tangmere Wing had lost its most famous commander when Bader was taken prisoner, its work continued. One of the pilots doing that work was a young, inexperienced member of No 616 Squadron from Westhampnett who had seen Bader go down. This was Pilot Officer 'Johnnie' Johnson, who would go on to have one of the most spectacular careers of any Sussex RAF man.

Johnson had been born in Leicestershire in 1915 and, wanting to go to university, bought a shotgun with which to shoot rabbits and wildfowl to sell for cash to pay his bills. Johnson would later ascribe his astonishingly accurate shooting from a Spitfire to this practice on the ground. He worked his way through Nottingham University to graduate as an engineer in 1937. He joined up as soon as war was declared and in September 1940 joined No 616 Squadron on Spitfires. Almost at once he was taken off combat flying, due to a fractured collarbone. He did not therefore join operations from Westhampnett until the spring of 1941.

Johnson remained in Sussex until July 1942, by which time his score was up to a dozen confirmed kills. He was then given command of No 610 Squadron in Norfolk. It was at this point that Johnson began his practice of refusing to share in the credit for kills. He reasoned that less experienced pilots needed the boost to their confidence that an undisputed victory would bring, while he himself needed no such boost. As a result it is now impossible to know exactly what damage Johnson did to the Luftwaffe.

Johnnie Johnson in his Spitfire in the autumn of 1941. The Tangmere Wing had become known as 'The Bader Bus Company', so Johnson added the words 'Still Running' to his nose art after Bader was shot down and captured.

In March 1943 Johnson moved to Kenley in Surrey to take over No 403 Squadron, manned almost exclusively by Canadian pilots. In September he was taken off combat duties and given a staff job. His rest was not to last, for in February 1944 the Royal Canadian Air Force formed its own wing in Lincolnshire. So popular had Johnson been at No 403 that the Canadians demanded he be given command of the new unit, and Johnson then adopted

Johnnie Johnson climbing out of Spitfire at Tangmere. Only a young pilot among many others in 1941, Johnson went on to be the top scoring fighter pilot in Fighter Command.

142

the distinctive Canadian shoulder flash as a tribute to his men.

After D-Day, Johnson led his wing to France, where they spent some weeks camped out at temporary airfields. The rations were poor, so Johnson arranged a number of informal flights back over the sea to his old contacts in Sussex to pick up fresh fruit, vegetables and even a lobster to eke out supplies. It was when flying out of a French airfield that Johnson was hit for the first and only time during the war, his Spitfire being damaged but not downed. It was also here that he got his 38th confirmed kill, making him the RAF's top scoring pilot of the war.

Johnson chose to stay in the RAF after the war, with the rank of Wing Commander. In 1947 he was seconded to Canada to head up the RCAF staff college. He served in Korea, then in Germany, and in 1957 finally came back to Britain to command RAF Cottesmore. He eventually achieved the rank of Air Vice Marshal as head of the RAF's Middle East Command. Among the various medals awarded to Johnson were a DSO and two Bars, a DFC and Bar, a CBE and CV. The Americans awarded him the American DFC, Air Medal and Legion of Merit, while the Belgians gave him the Croix de Guerre and the Order of Leopold, and the French the Legion d'Honneur. He died in 2001.

Of course, other sections of Fighter Command continued to operate. The night fighters still went up to counter the nocturnal bombers sent over from France. After April 1941 there was a dramatic drop in the number of German bombers coming over Britain at night. At first this puzzled the RAF and its pilots. On 22 June the reason became clear when Germany and Rumania invaded Soviet Russia. The Luftwaffe had needed its main strength in the East to pound Russian defences.

Other squadrons and units were also in action. At Tangmere a mysterious special duty unit took up residence early in 1941. This unit had Westland Lysanders that were painted completely black and operated without markings of any kind. They flew only at night and, although the unit's pilots and groundcrew mixed with the other RAF men at Tangmere, they stayed very tight-lipped about what they did. In fact they were dropping supplies and agents into occupied Europe, mostly France. The very short take-off and landing distance needed by the Lysander made it ideal for using small fields as clandestine landing spots.

Although not part of Fighter Command, these special duty units did impact on fighter pilots, as Tangmere's Squadron Leader Patrick Gibbs was to find out in July 1941. Like Bader, Gibbs was considerably older than most of the pilots flying with Fighter Command. He had joined the RAF in 1933 and had spent most of the war as a flying instructor teaching new fighter pilots the skills needed to dogfight. He was to find his mastery of aerobatics very useful on 9 July 1941.

Gibbs was flying with the Tangmere Wing on a ramrod raid, escorting bombers to Mazingarbe in France, when the formation was bounced by Messerschmitt Bf 109s near Le Touquet. Gibbs set one Bf 109 on fire in a head-on attack, but did not see a second German get on his tail until it was too late. The Spitfire's engine seized up as glycol poured out.

Glancing round, Gibbs saw the Bf 109 closing in for the kill. Believing that if he took to his parachute, the German was likely to machine gun him to death, Gibbs flipped his Spitfire on to its back and began gliding down toward the ground upside down. The Bf 109 followed him for a while, then broke off, apparently believing that Gibbs was dead. A few feet from the ground, Gibbs righted his aircraft and rolled to a bumpy, but safe landing.

Getting out of the Spitfire, Gibbs performed his first duty of setting fire

Armourers inspect ammunition for the 20 mm cannon introduced to British fighters in 1941. The exploding shells of the weapon proved to be massively effective against enemy aircraft.

to the aircraft so that it did not fall into enemy hands. Then he set off to get away from the site before German troops arrived. As evening drew in, he risked knocking on a farmhouse door. He received a warm welcome, some food and a bed for the night. The farmer knew nothing about the Resistance, however, so Gibbs moved on next day. The second evening he tried his luck at a second farm, where again he was fed and allowed to rest. The farmer contacted a local doctor who 'would know what to do'. He did. Gibbs was given an address in Paris and some money to help him get there. The Paris flat turned out to be home to a girl student who was part of a joint enterprise between the French Resistance and the British Secret Service to get downed RAF flyers out of occupied Europe.

Known by the codename of the Pat Line, this organisation had begun in July 1940 when Captain Ian Garrow of the Seaforth Highlanders got cut off in the retreat to Dunkirk. Garrow then met up with Captain Harold Cole, another Dunkirk refugee. The two men travelled to Marseille, then in Vichy France, and contacted the British Special Operations Executive (SOE), who put them in touch with a Belgian army officer, Albert Guerisse, who used the codename Patrick O'Leary. The three men then went back over the route used by Cole and Garrow to formalise it and recruit people willing to provide safe houses, forge papers and generally help evaders on the run. Only later did it transpire that Cole was really a wanted man, having stolen his regimental pay chest and fled during the chaos of the retreat to Dunkirk.

The Paris student gave Gibbs forged identity papers and travel permits. She then accompanied him south to Perpignan in Vichy France on the pretext that he was her fiancé and that she was taking him to introduce him to her aunt. In Perpignan, a local man was waiting at the aunt's house. He gave Gibbs instructions on how to walk to Spain and the next day he set off with a pocketful of change to buy food en route.

Gibbs had almost made it, when a French policeman stopped him and asked to see his papers. Gibbs produced them, but the policeman spotted they were forgeries and arrested him on suspicion of unspecified crimes. Gibbs revealed who he really was and asked the policeman to let him go. The policeman refused and handcuffed Gibbs before sending him to an internment camp near Nimes.

Gibbs managed to escape on 18 August and set off to walk to the address of a safe house he had been given in case of emergency. From there a Frenchman directed him back to Perpignan to a different safe house, where he met four other Allied servicemen who were in the hands of the Pat Line.

The five men set off with a local guide a few days later for the arduous walk to Spain. They got over a high pass at 10,000 ft, evading the dozing French sentry on duty, and were then picked up by a Spanish guide who led them to Barcelona. In that city the five men went to see the British Consul, who arranged for them to travel to Gibraltar, from where they were flown home. Gibbs had been away for three months and had been posted as 'missing, believed killed'.

The Pat Line continued to operate until March 1943, getting over 600 Allied airmen and escaped prisoners of war to safety in Spain. Then Cole was captured by the Gestapo and to save his life betrayed the entire organisation. Over 100 French men and women were arrested and most of them executed by the Germans. Garrow got out alive, while Albert Guerisse was treated as a prisoner of war, though only after the Gestapo had tortured him but failed to get any new information. Cole was released by the Germans, then shot dead by the French Resistance.

In September 1941 two factors intervened to bring an end to the hectic months of sweeps over France. The first was the advent of winter with its long nights, bad weather and poor light. These would, in any case, have curtailed major daylight operations over France. The second factor was the sudden appearance of a new type of German fighter.

A pilot of No 609 Squadron came back from a sweep to report that he had been faced by a new type of Bf 109. He said that the new model had a radial engine, as opposed to the in-line engine of the existing Bf 109 models. RAF Intelligence were alerted and interviewed the pilot, but quickly dismissed his sighting as a mistake. They knew from studying crashed Bf 109s that the air frame was totally unsuitable for a radial engine.

Nevertheless, reports continued to come in from RAF pilots of this radial-engined fighter. Some thought it a version of Bf 109, others that it was a new type altogether. Whatever it was, this new fighter was reported to be faster than a conventional Bf 109. By November, Intelligence was forced to accept that a new German fighter was patrolling the skies over France and that it was superior even to the Spitfire.

Eventually the RAF learned what this new fighter was. It was the Focke Wulf Fw 190.

Focke Wulf Fw 190

Type: Fighter
Engine: 1 x 1700 hp
BMW 801D
Wingspan: 34 ft 5 in
Length: 29 ft
Height: 13 ft
Weight: Empty 6393 lb
Loaded 8770 lb
Armament: 2 x 7.9 machine guns in
nose plus 4 x 20 mm
cannon in wings
Max speed: 382 mph
Ceiling: 35,000 ft
Range: 500 miles
Production: 20,051

The Focke Wulf Fw 190 was far superior to any other fighter in the world when it entered service in 1941. Its Luftwaffe pilots nicknamed it 'Der Würger', meaning Butcher Bird.

Without doubt Germany's finest fighter of the war, the Focke Wulf Fw 190 first flew in June 1939 but problems with the engine meant it did not enter combat in significant numbers until the end of 1941. It proved to be fast and nimble, easily outclassing all Allied fighters – even the Spitfire MkV, which had only just entered service. The British rushed the Spitfire IX into production, but this took time and only matched the Fw 190 in combat conditions. By the end of 1942 half of all German fighters being produced were Fw 190s, designed in a number of variants to carry bombs or torpedoes as well as the standard fighter armament. In 1944 a variant, the Fw 190D, was produced with a Junkers Jumo 213 engine. This aircraft proved to be a magnificent high-altitude fighter and took a heavy toll of American daylight bombers operating above 30,000 feet. The Fw 190G was a ground attack variant, able to carry up to 4000 lbs of bombs to a range of 220 miles from base.

Chapter 8

On the Back Foot

The winter of 1941/42 was spent quietly by Fighter Command. The advent of the Focke Wulf Fw 190 had made sweeps over northern France highly dangerous affairs that offered few benefits. Only ramrods against vital targets and rhubarbs in favourable circumstances were flown. But if the end of 1941 was bad for Fighter Command, the start of 1942 was to be even worse, with the greatest fiasco of the war.

The German pocket battleships, technically battlecruisers, *Scharnhorst* and *Gneisenau* had long been the most potent threat to the Atlantic convoys. Each of the two ships was armed with nine 11 inch guns plus a mass of anti-aircraft weapons and secondary armament. At full speed they could top 31 knots and had armour up to 14 inches thick. If they found a convoy, they could sink it in minutes.

The two battlecruisers had taken part in the invasion of Norway, sinking a British aircraft carrier and two destroyers as well as fighting a British battlecruiser to a draw. In January 1941 they steamed into the Atlantic, sinking 22 merchant ships and forcing every convoy at sea to head for the nearest port and all convoys in harbour to stay put. The Royal Navy constantly worried that the two ships, berthed in Brest, would again put to sea to play havoc among the convoy routes.

The RAF had been called in to try to bomb the two battlecruisers to destruction. Raid after raid was launched on Brest by RAF Bomber

Command, with Fighter Command's 10 Group providing escorts. Swift reactions by Luftwaffe fighters and accurate flak over Brest meant that no serious damage was done to the ships, though the harbour facilities were badly hit. In December 1941 raids by commandos convinced Hitler that the British were about to try an invasion of northern Norway; so he ordered the navy to bring the two battlecruisers back from Brest to Kiel.

The British were aware that the Germans might try to get the two ships back to Germany, and had plans in place. If the ships sought to steer north around Scotland, they would be handled by the Navy; if they tried to go up the Channel, they would be the target of the RAF. The codeword for the operation to stop them was Fuller, and all the squadrons of the RAF, both bomber and fighter, had a role to play. It was assumed that the Germans would time their run to pass through the narrow seas between Dover and Calais in darkness.

As night fell on 11 February 1942, the German naval crews went into action. The weather forecast was for unremittingly bad weather for at least 24 hours, which the Germans hoped would give them cover from the RAF. Crucially, the German plan called for them to leave Brest at night, when they would be unobserved, even though this would put them off Dover in daylight.

When the usual high-flying dawn reconnaissance flight sent out from Britain arrived over Brest next day it was to find solid cloud cover. Nothing could be seen. Meanwhile the long-range aircraft of Coastal Command that was patrolling the western entrance to the English Channel suffered a breakdown of its air to surface radar. By the time a replacement had taken off and arrived on station, the German ships had slipped past. Ground-based radar in England picked up the array of small ships escorting the two giants, but these were dismissed as being an E-boat patrol.

Meanwhile Squadron Leader R. Oxspring of No 91 Squadron at Tangmere had gone up to investigate a radar report of German aircraft over Le Touquet. No Fighter Command operations were due that day, so Oxspring had the skies to himself as he pushed through the murk and cloud. Oxspring came out of the cloud cover off Le Touquet to find himself confronted by a vast whirling mass of circling German fighters. Peering down to see what

The German pocket battleship Scharnhorst, *photographed in Brest by the RAF in 1941. The subsequent escape of this warship and its sister ship the* Gneisenau *was deeply embarrassing for the RAF.*

the Germans were guarding, Oxspring saw the *Scharnhorst* and *Gneisenau* together with their escorting ships. He hurriedly radioed the news back to base, then dived into cloud before the German fighters could catch him.

Thus it was at 11.30 am that a Fighter Command officer telephoned Bomber Command to alert them of the need to implement Operation Fuller. Unfortunately both the head of Bomber Command, then Air Vice Marshal Jack Baldwin, and his deputy were in a car on the way to a conference at the Air Ministry and could not be contacted. A rather gallant staff officer of lowly squadron leader rank took it upon himself to issue the instructions to get things moving.

Squadrons throughout southern England were scrambled into the air. Unfortunately, all the RAF plans had been drawn up assuming that the German ships would be spotted hours before they got off the Sussex coast, never mind off Le Touquet. Squadron Leader Humphrey Gilbert out of Westhampnett was escorting a force of bombers on a raid to attack the ships. The force failed to find the ships, let alone attack them, but they in their turn were found by a squadron of Bf 109s. In the fighting that followed Gilbert managed to shoot down one Bf 109 and damage another. This

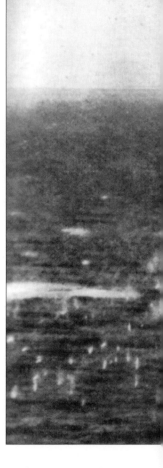

was his fifth confirmed victory since he first flew a Spitfire into combat in August 1940.

In all, 242 bombers took off that day, escorted by a cloud of fighters sent up from Tangmere and other stations. Given the bad weather, the lack of warning and the position of the warships, most RAF aircraft failed to find their targets. Eugene Desmond and six torpedo bombers of the Fleet Air Arm did find the ships and attacked, but all six aircraft were shot down. The only damage suffered by the ships came when the *Scharnhorst* hit a mine off Holland.

The embarrassing failure to halt the Channel dash was all the worse as it came at a time when the Japanese were capturing Malaya, Singapore and

A ship is hit by cannon fire from a patrolling Beaufighter. German coastal shipping continued to be a target off occupied France throughout 1943.

Hong Kong, as well as sweeping through the Dutch East Indies and the Philippines. It seemed as if the British could not even control their own backyard. There followed an inquiry into the debacle. While the bulk of the blame was laid on sheer bad luck, the lack of close liaison between 11 Group of Fighter Command and Coastal Command was highlighted. Nobody came out of it very well.

For the men and women based at Tangmere the humiliation of the Channel dash was, in part at least, alleviated by a visit from the entire company of

A sequence of three shots taken by the gun cameras of a Spitfire when attacking a Messerschmitt Bf 109 over France. The German aircraft is hit on its left wing root in the top photo, quickly catching fire in the subsequent pictures.

the Windmill Theatre in London. Two shows were staged starring the Crazy Gang, Bud Flanagan and a full supporting cast. It was a huge event for the airbase.

Meanwhile, Fighter Command was struggling to cope with the Focke Wulf Fw 190. The Spitfire Mk V, then the standard model, was too slow and lacked acceleration and climb, particularly at altitude. Fortunately Rolls-Royce had recently produced an uprated Merlin engine with two superchargers and a strengthened engine block able to produce greater power. Supermarine hurriedly redesigned the front end of the Spitfire V to accommodate the new engine and designated the result the Mk IX. This Mk IX would prove to be the equal of the Fw 190, though each had its strengths and weaknesses in combat. Unfortunately the new Spitfire would not be ready to enter production until July 1942 and would not be available in numbers until the autumn.

The first real test of the Spitfire Mk IX came with the Dieppe raid of August 1942. This was designed to be a one-day operation with the dual purpose of inflicting massive damage on the German-occupied port and of testing out the ideas about amphibious landings then taking shape. In essence it was a small scale trial for the invasion of France that would finally happen as D-Day on 6 June 1944.

The Dieppe raid took place on 19 August and proved to be a disaster. Operational problems led to poor co-operation between the navy and army, and insufficient reconnaissance saw heavy attacks on unimportant targets while vital objectives were missed out altogether. Over half the mostly Canadian troops who landed became casualties and the tank force was wiped out.

In contrast to the Channel dash fiasco, however, Fighter Command came out of the raid rather well. The new Spitfire Mk IX was used in large numbers, as was the older Spitfire Mk V. It was found that aircraft to aircraft, the Spitfire Mk IX had the edge over the Fw 190 above 23,000 ft, but that the German fighter was better below that altitude. But the efficient and effective rota employed by Fighter Command to

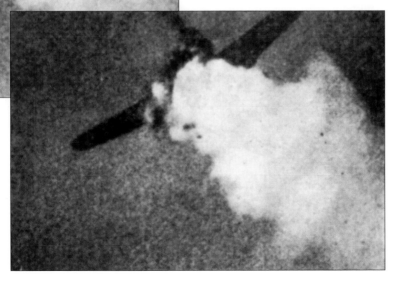

send over wing after wing to a carefully co-ordinated timetable meant that fresh aircraft were always over Dieppe. The RAF won and maintained air supremacy over the town throughout the operation.

In the wake of the Dieppe raid, Air Vice Marshal Trafford Leigh-Mallory was promoted to take command of Fighter Command. This had been his ambition for years and he threw himself into the task wholeheartedly. In November 1944 he was to be killed in an accidental air crash and replaced by Air Marshal Sir Roderic Hill.

These two major operations apart, Fighter Command continued during 1942 with the steady programme of other duties. The advent of the Fw 190 led to a reduction in the number of rhubarbs, circuses and rodeos, as the risks came to outweigh the gains. Ramrods, however, continued to take place to attack important targets. New tactics were developed to help escort ramrods. To ensure that the fighters had the fuel necessary for dogfights at any stage of the mission, it became normal for one fighter force to escort the bombers out and another to escort them back, while a third force rendezvoused with the bombers over the target to provide additional cover during the bombing runs.

One Westhampnett pilot managed to down a Bf 109 in most unusual circumstances during a ramrod near Dunkirk in October 1942. Sergeant Wilfred Palmer had been engaged in dogfights over France for some time, running out of ammunition entirely and also becoming low on fuel. As he turned for home

In 1942 R.F. Hamlin (below) became head of the RAF's Air-Sea rescue service. Many pilots of Fighter Command would owe their lives to his efficient organisation by the end of the war. Here (opposite) a fighter pilot is about to be rescued from his dinghy by the crew of a flying boat.

he was alarmed to see three German fighters diving down on him from a great height. He put his Spitfire's nose down for speed, but it was clear that the Germans would catch up with him before he reached the French coast, never mind making it to Britain.

With no ammunition left, Palmer could not fight, so he went right down to ground level and began 'hedge-hopping' in the hope that he would shake

off his pursuers. Flying at over 300 mph at such low level leaves little time for mistakes. As Palmer conducted his heart-stopping race, he saw a pylon looming into view. Realising that this indicated the presence of electricity cables, he put his Spitfire down as low as he dared and roared under the wires. One of the German pilots was less lucky, crashing into the cables and disappearing in a ball of flame as his aircraft exploded. The other two Germans broke off the pursuit and Palmer was able to reach Westhampnett safely.

After August 1942 Tangmere occasionally played host to secret missions flown by men of No 264 and No 515 Squadrons. They were based elsewhere but came to Tangmere for refuelling and preparation when they needed to operate over the Channel south of Sussex. These missions were flown by the aging Boulton Paul Defiant turret fighters that had not been seen in action since the winter of 1940/41. They were no longer fighters, however, but specialist aircraft packed full of high-tech electronic equipment codenamed 'Moonshine' and 'Mandrel'.

Mandrel was a system that jammed German radar systems. It worked over only a small area, and several Defiants would be sent up to patrol tightly defined routes so as to jam the German radar over as wide an area as possible. Moonshine, on the other hand, gave the impression to German radar operators that the single Defiant was up to a hundred aircraft flying in formation. Aircraft on Moonshine missions would follow routes at speeds mimicking a bomber formation heading for a particular target. At the last minute, they would switch off their equipment and race for home. They were potentially hazardous missions which continued off and on until July 1943.

As the good weather of spring and summer took hold, the Germans stepped up their fast daylight raids by fighter-bomber versions of the Messerschmitt Me 110 and Bf 109. Later in the year bomber versions of the Fw 190 began to appear, carrying up to 1,000 lbs of bombs under the fuselage. The raids these planes made were usually on a small scale and aimed at ports or coastal towns and targets. Occasionally, however, they were on a larger scale, with airfields, factories or other specified targets as their objective.

In April 1942 there began what the British called the Baedeker raids by

A squadron sets out on a sweep over France in the summer of 1942, watched by a farm worker. By this date fighter sweeps were becoming increasingly dangerous operations.

The first photo of the Mosquito to be released to the public. This is a prototpye bomber version but the aircraft was also available in fighter and nightfighter versions by the summer of 1942.

the Luftwaffe. These started in April and lasted through until October. They took their name from the fact that the German bombers struck at towns or cities noted for their cultural and architectural links rather than industrial importance. The elegant Georgian city of Bath was a typical target. The British assumed that the Germans were choosing their targets from the pages of the pre-war *Baedeker* tourist guide to Britain. These nocturnal raids kept the night fighters active, along with anti-aircraft guns and searchlight batteries.

Some of the night fighters based in Sussex specialised in what would become known as 'intruder' missions. These involved taking off at dusk and flying out to France to lurk around Luftwaffe bases in the hope of finding a target. Airfields marked out their runways with lights when bombers were taking off or landing, and the bombers themselves often showed lights at these times of their mission. Intruder missions did not, generally, achieve great results at this date, but they did serve to unnerve the Germans and force them to douse their lights if the drone of unfriendly engines was heard.

Among the most outstanding intruders in Fighter Command were Tangmere's Sergeant Leonard Langley and his pilot Sergeant John Raffels, who flew with No 23 Squadron. At the end of 1942, when the squadron left Tangmere to retrain to fly Mosquitoes, the pair were awarded a DFM each. They had by this time shot down a confirmed three enemy bombers at night, plus one probable, and had attacked Luftwaffe airfields on twelve occasions. The citation recorded that both men had 'shown outstanding courage and initiative in every sortie and are a shining example to all concerned'.

Less fortunate was the No 23 squadron partnership of Sergeant Peter Roberts and his pilot, Flying Officer Philip Ensor. They too shot down three enemy bombers, as well as destroying a fourth on the ground during an intruder mission. Roberts was awarded a DFM and Ensor, being an officer, a DFC. During a mission on 8 September 1942 their aircraft was shot down and both men were killed.

The achievements of both these crews were, however, outstripped by another crew in No 23 Squadron: Sergeant Roy Sherrington and pilot Wing Commander Bertie Hoare. Hoare had already been awarded a DFC for his work in 1940, but now with Sergeant Sherrington took to intruder work with a passion. During their time at Tangmere they flew no less than 40

Under a full moon the air crew of a night-fighter squadron wait beside a Mosquito to get the order to take off to meet an incoming German raid.

A Mosquito NFII sits on the tarmac at sunset. This was the most numerous night-fighter version of the Mosquito in 1943, with 270 having been built.

intruder sorties, cruising around the night skies over occupied France in search of targets. They shot down a confirmed three German aircraft, with four probables, and launched numerous attacks on airfields and other ground targets. They were known in their squadron for a winning combination of coolness and efficiency.

When No 23 Squadron left Tangmere their night fighter role in Sussex was taken over by No 29 Squadron moving into Ford airfield with Mosquitoes. The crews of No 29 Squadron were not allowed to fly intruder missions by direct order of Leigh-Mallory. The reason for this was that the aircraft were equipped with a new version of air-to-air radar that he did not want to fall into German hands. The aircrew resented the limitation, but accepted it.

The restriction seems not to have curtailed the exploits of No 29 Squadron's star crew, Sergeant Joseph Toone and pilot Flying Officer George Pepper. In just six months this crew shot down a confirmed six German bombers by night, and damaged several more. In August they were stalking a Junkers Ju 88 through a cloudy night when the aircraft vanished from Toone's radar screen. Unperturbed, Toone proceeded to give Pepper directions based on what he guessed would be the German's evasive manoeuvres. Coming out of a cloud, Pepper saw the Ju 88 exactly where Toone had predicted it would be and shot it down.

Toone was later promoted to be a pilot officer and was awarded a DFC to go with his DFM, one of the very few men in the RAF to win both medals.

The year 1942 was important for Fighter Command, as it saw the introduction of a new type of aircraft: the Mosquito. This wooden aircraft had been developed by the de Havilland company to be a fast bomber that relied on its speed and altitude for safety rather than on its defensive guns. It became clear during development that the fast, agile aircraft would also make a good fighter if suitably adapted.

The first Mosquito fighter entered service in January 1942, very quickly followed by a night fighter version with air-to-air radar. The Mosquito was significantly faster than the Beaufighter, with a better climb rate and more nimble movements. The Beaufighter would continue to prowl the night skies until 1944, but by 1943 it had been overtaken in terms of numbers by the Mosquito.

The Tangmere night fighters continued to fly their Beaufighters throughout 1942. In July, Sergeant William Clarke of No 219 Squadron celebrated a full year with the squadron by shooting down his fourth enemy night bomber. The event was marked by his being awarded a DFM for what was described as 'considerable ability that has been an example to the rest of the squadron'.

As 1942 turned to 1943 the duties of Fighter Command remained much as they had been, though with subtle changes. The war in the air was gradually being won by the Allies. Although the Luftwaffe remained a constant threat, the daylight skies over Europe were no longer a suicide mission for Allied bombers. This was especially true if the bombers were flying within fighter range of Britain.

Nor were missions into Continental skies any longer a matter of looking for something to hit or hoping that the Luftwaffe came up to be ambushed. An increasing flow of information from both resistance workers in occupied countries and high-level reconnaissance flights meant that the Allied air planners increasingly knew where useful targets were to be found. Added to that was the growing realisation that 1944 would be the year when the Western Allies invaded France, and would bring the need to hit specific targets to make the invasion an easier task. The summer of 1943 saw missions flown with a purpose and to achieve specific results. The old freewheeling rhubarb days were gone for ever.

Also becoming rather more focused were the clandestine flights made by the Lysanders of Tangmere's No 161 Squadron. In 1942 they had averaged about ten flights to France each month. In 1943 three times as many flights were made. No 161 was not the only squadron flying such missions. No 138 Squadron had Halifaxes for flying more long distance missions or to drop

The Spitfire Mk XII had clipped wingtips to improve performance at low altitudes and a Griffon IV engine. It was introduced in February 1943, specifically to counter low-level hit and run raids by bomber variants of the Fw 190. Only 100 of this model were built to fill this specific role.

heavy loads of supplies. No 138 was stationed elsewhere, but one of their number made an unscheduled stop at Tangmere in the summer of 1943.

Sergeant John Tweed was flying in a Halifax that had dropped stores to a Resistance group in southern France when he was shot down over Troyes. The aircraft crashlanded, injuring all on board. Tweed dragged the worst injured from the wreck, then hobbled off on a sprained ankle to find cover. He saw an ambulance arrive to take away his comrades, but no search was made for him. The following night he made his way to a farm, where the French family gave him food, then ushered him off to a barn to sleep.

Tweed spent the next two weeks in the barn. He was visited by a local doctor and interrogated by a mysterious Frenchman who arrived and left unannounced. This turned out to be Louis Joubin of the French Resistance, who radioed Tweed's story to London to ensure he was not a Gestapo man pretending to be RAF in order to infiltrate the Resistance. Reassured, Joubin arranged forged identity papers for Tweed and had him moved to a safe house in the form of a café in a small village near Troyes.

A few days later Tweed was moved to a flat in Paris, home to Henri Boucher. There was then a hold up while Boucher tried to make arrangements for Tweed to be sent south along an established route for evaders known as the Marie-Claire Line. One problem after another cropped up and Tweed spent nine weeks living in a single tiny room overlooking Montmartre. Finally an Englishman dressed in French civilian clothes arrived and told Tweed that they were leaving in less than an hour.

Tweed was led by his taciturn new contact to a railway station and together they went to Angers, where they were met by a French farmer with a pair of bicycles. The two Englishmen then cycled to an anonymous field to be met by four others. Only then did Tweed's companion reveal that he was Captain Ben Cowburn of the SOE. After dark, local French Resistance fighters turned up with some flares. When the sounds of engines were heard the flares were lit and laid out to mark a safe landing strip in the field.

Down came two Lysanders from Tangmere piloted by Flying Officer Jimmy Bathgate and Wing Commander Bob Hodges, himself an RAF man who had escaped from France with the help of the Resistance and SOE. Tweed and his fellow evaders were flown back to Tangmere, where they once again set foot on English soil. Tweed had been away more than four months. The flight that picked him up was just routine for Tangmere's Lysander pilots.

The commander of the unit was Group Captain Hugh Verity, a pre-war teacher with a flair for languages. After flying night fighters for a while, Verity served at Fighter Command HQ. He was then very keen to return to operations and met Wing Commander Pickard, who thought his experience of night flying and ability to speak French made him ideal for the SOE.

Late in 1943 Verity was given the task of flying Jean Moulin, head of General de Gaulle's Free French Resistance, to a landing strip in the Loire Valley. The outbound flight was uneventful, though made at the usual hair-raising low altitude in total darkness, but when Verity reached the landing strip it was covered in fog, so the landing had to be aborted. On the way back to Tangmere, Verity ran into an unexpected German searchlight and anti-aircraft battery which gave him some trouble.

Finally arriving over Tangmere, Verity came in to land his Lysander. But what Verity took to be the ground was, in fact, the top of a layer of ground mist so when he put the aircraft down to land he was really about 30 ft up. The resulting 'prang' destroyed the Lysander, though neither Verity nor Moulin was badly hurt. As he helped his passenger out of the wreckage

The aircrew of a Mosquito night fighter squadron are given their final briefing before taking off for the night's mission protecting Britain from nocturnal Luftwaffe bombers.

Verity apologised profusely in French, only for Moulin to thank him in broken English for 'a very agreeable flight'.

In 1944 Verity was promoted to supervise clandestine air operations against the Japanese in Burma, where he stayed for the rest of the war. In 1948 he was given command of No 541 Squadron, a Spitfire unit and then in 1955 he was given a squadron of modern fighter jets. He retired in 1965 and died in 2001.

When Verity left Tangmere, his old squadron was busier than they had ever been. They were soon to be even busier as the countdown to D-Day began.

Junkers Ju 88

Type:	Four-crew bomber
Engines:	2 x 1200 hp Junkers Jumo 211B
Wingspan:	59 ft 11 in
Length:	7 ft 2 in
Height:	5 ft 10 in
Weight:	Empty 21,717 lb
	Loaded 30,865 lb
Armament:	6 x 7.9 2mm machine guns in nose, dorsal and ventral positions plus 4400 lb of bombs
Max speed:	292 mph
Ceiling:	26,900 ft
Range:	1696 miles
Production:	7000

During the war the Germans built more of the Junkers Ju 88 than of any other aircraft. It was intended as a bomber, but was subsequently built in dozens of different models for night fighting, ground attack, maritime reconnaisance, tank busting and a variety of other uses.

The Junkers Ju 88 was designed as a high-speed medium bomber in 1936, and it was this early variant of the Ju 88 that featured most in the Battle of Britain. This 88A was designed to be able to carry a fairly heavy bombload on conventional level bombing missions, but also to be able to deliver a lighter bombload when dive-bombing. It entered service with the Luftwaffe in August 1939, but was not used much in the Polish campaign, as the crews were still getting used to its handling characteristics. It entered combat on 26 September with an attack on British shipping off the Scottish coast and thereafter was seen in increasingly large numbers over the Western Front. The Ju 88 was later produced in a bewilderingly large number of variants and models, totalling 15,000 aircraft in all. There were torpedo bombers, night fighters, reconnaissance aircraft, maritime patrol bombers and ground attack versions. Production continued right up until the day before the Americans captured the Junkers factory in March 1945.

De Havilland Mosquito

Type:	Twin-engined, two-seat fighter
Engine:	2 x 1460 hp Rolls-Royce Merlin 23
Wingspan:	54 ft 2 in
Length:	41 ft 9 in
Height:	15 ft 3 in
Weight:	Empty 14,300 lb Loaded 20,000 lb
Armament:	4 x 20 mm cannon in nose plus 4 x .303 in machine guns
Max speed:	407 mph
Ceiling:	39,000 ft
Range:	1770 miles (with drop tanks)
Production:	1579

A fighter Mosquito. When this wooden aircraft appeared its speed and agility were a revelation. With four cannon and four machine guns in the nose it packed a powerful punch. (Paul Lazell)

The Mosquito was originally conceived as a fast bomber, but its superlative performance meant that even before the bomber version entered production a fighter version was being developed. It entered service early in 1942, but a lack of numbers meant that it had little impact on air combat until 1943. The formidable punch of the nose-mounted armament and its great speed made this a highly effective fighter. In March 1943 a radar-equipped night fighter version began to be produced. The machine guns were taken out to make space for the radar, but the remaining four cannon proved perfectly adequate. Various models of the night fighter were built, with different radars producing a variety of nose shapes for this aircraft. It remained in active service until 1950.

Chapter 9

The Invasion of Europe

The spring and summer of 1944 would prove to be the busiest period of the war for Fighter Command in Sussex, outstripping even the hectic days of the Battle of Britain. The reason was, of course, the D-Day invasion of Europe. Located directly north of the Normandy beaches, Sussex was the ideal launch pad for air missions and offered the closest airfields – always a consideration for short-range aircraft such as fighters.

A Hawker Typhoon goes into action in 1944. The early career of the Typhoon was marred by unreliable engines.

171

Among those fighters was a new addition to Fighter Command's arsenal: the Hawker Typhoon. With a choice of either twelve machine guns or four cannon, the Typhoon was designed to be a hard-hitting bomber destroyer able to top 400 mph. However, problems with the Sabre engine delayed production so long that by the time it was ready for operations the worst of the Luftwaffe bombing raids were over. Experience soon showed that at anything over 18,000 ft it was too heavy to match either the Messerschmitt Bf 109 or Focke Wulf Fw 190 for agility. Since achieving air control now rested on defeating those fighters at high altitude, the Typhoon seemed redundant.

However, below 14,000 ft, the Typhoon was a clear match for the German fighters so it could cope well with the task of flying close escort for Allied bombers in daylight. And it was the perfecting of air-to-ground rockets late in 1943 that turned the Typhoon into a truly awesome weapon of war. This big, powerful fighter could carry eight rockets as well as its more conventional armament, so it could act as a ground-attack and fighter aircraft at the same time. The rockets could be fired in pairs or all at once, concentrating as much explosive fire power as the broadside of a naval cruiser. Firing rockets proved to be even more accurate than dive bombing. The Typhoon would go on to become a much feared sight for the German army, able to blow apart even the largest tanks with ease.

First, however, a great deal of preliminary work was necessary. In November 1943 Fighter Command officially ceased to exist. In its place emerged two new organisations within the RAF. The first of these was named the Air Defence of Great Britain (ADGB). As its name suggests, this consisted of those units whose tasks were solely concerned with defending the air space over Britain itself. It embraced the searchlight, balloon and anti-aircraft batteries as well as the night fighter squadrons and those day squadrons detailed to protect Britain.

The second new command was the 2nd Tactical Air Force (2nd TAF). This was made up of those Fighter Command squadrons that had been chiefly engaged in sweeps or intruder missions over occupied Europe. To these squadrons were added a few light and medium bomber squadrons from Bomber Command. The role of 2nd TAF was initially to pound targets in occupied Europe, mostly in preparation for the invasion. Once the invasion had taken place they were to move over to airfields in Europe, following the armies on their planned advance to Germany and the heart of the Reich. Meanwhile, they were based in Sussex and nearby areas.

Captured by the gun camera of a Spitfire, a Luftwaffe pilot bales out of his crippled Focke Wulfe Fw 190 over France. By 1944 new versions of Allied fighter had largely negated the advantage of the Fw 190 in combat.

It was clear that the existing fighter airfields of Tangmere, Ford and Westhampnett in Sussex would be unable to cope with the large number of aircraft expected to operate from the county. The need for additional airfields had been recognised after the Dieppe raid. On that occasion Fighter Command had gained and held air supremacy over the town and the sea offshore, but only by putting up vast numbers of fighters on a strict rota system. To be confident of achieving air supremacy in the much larger area over the Normandy beaches and English Channel would require far more aircraft, even given the depleted state of the Luftwaffe by the summer of 1944. It was to provide bases for these aircraft that the advanced landing grounds (ALGs) were constructed.

The ALGs were never intended to be permanent airfields. The runways were constructed of heavy-duty metal mesh laid down over the turf, while accommodation consisted of requisitioned nearby houses and tents. There were to be four hangars at each ALG, but again these were temporary constructions, known as blister hangars. Care was taken over selecting the sites, the ideal being a flat area of poor-grade farmland close to woodland, where stores could be hidden from probing Luftwaffe eyes. There were not enough such sites to be found in Sussex, so some good quality farmland had to be sacrificed, much to the annoyance of the local farmers.

Among the unsung heroes of Fighter Command were the runway repair crews of the ALGs. The metal spikes holding the runway mesh in position were constantly working loose, so the men had to rush out to hammer them back in at short notice. More than once they were at work even as aircraft came into land, the men scattering for a few seconds, then returning to their task.

In December 1942 workmen started to clear a site just outside Bognor Regis, flattening out bumps and demolishing farm buildings in line with the runways. January 1943 saw work begin at Chailey, and in February at Selsey, Apuldram and Coolham. Cowdray Park had been a private airfield used by Lord Cowdray and his friends before the war, so this needed only to have metal mesh laid down for it to become an ALG. It was July 1943 before work began at Deanland. A grass air strip at Funtingdon had been cleared early in the war as an emergency landing strip for damaged aircraft and it was upgraded to be an ALG in September 1943. Two months later the old army base at Hammerwood began conversion. A final ALG was planned to be built at Pulborough, but it was never constructed.

Even while the ALGs were being constructed, squadrons were being moved into Sussex, or new ones formed. Both the ADGB and 2nd TAF had bases in the county and the pace of activity quickened appreciably. The main targets for 2nd TAF were German military bases in northern France and the Low Countries, plus transportation links, railway locomotives and rolling stock, and factories producing military equipment. Although the primary need was to prepare for the landings in Normandy, it was necessary to launch raids as if preparing for an invasion taking place around Calais so as to mislead the Germans.

The ALGs had a second, but no less vital purpose as emergency landing grounds for damaged aircraft. Deanland received its first emergency visitor as the workmen were still laying the runway: a Spitfire came down in August 1943 as its wounded pilot felt he was about to pass out from loss of blood. The following month, by which time the runway was completed, a B17 Flying Fortress of the US 8th Air Force came in, the first of 19 that would land or crashland on the airfield.

Chailey went operational as an ALG on 24 April 1944 with No 18 (Polish)

Fighter Wing in residence. The wing had satellite bases at Coolham and Selsey, the latter in Dorset. It consisted of six Polish squadrons, one Belgian squadron and two British squadrons, but was always commanded by a Pole; in 1944 the commanding officer was Group Captain Alexsander Gabszewicz. Although the Poles were equipped by the RAF and integrated into the RAF structure, they retained their individual character and the aircraft all carried a distinctive red and white checked square to identify them.

The Poles' first action from Sussex was to escort American bombers to a target near Amiens on 27 April, a mission that passed off without incident. A similar mission to Dunkirk on 1 May saw Flying Officer Pentz return with his tailplane heavily damaged by flak, but he was unhurt. Thereafter the Poles were flying every day, either escorting bombers to France or flying air-sea rescue patrols over the Channel to try to locate downed airmen. The Spitfires were able to carry bombs and after 8 May the Poles concentrated on their own bombing attacks on railway junctions, airfields and bridges.

The Poles' first casualty since arriving in Sussex came on 18 May 1944 when the Spitfire engine of Flying Officer Adamek suddenly cut out over the Channel, probably due to a hit from German flak that had been encountered over the target at Fecamp. Adamek bailed out, but his parachute got tangled around the tail of his Spitfire and he was dragged down to his death.

While the Poles were settling in at Chailey and Coolham, Funtingdon was playing host to the Typhoon squadrons, Nos 164, 183, 198 and 609. Squadron Leader John Baldwin of No 609 Squadron had already been awarded a DFC for his work flying Spitfires in 1943. On one occasion he was bounced by three Bf 109s as he returned from a rhubarb over Belgium. He turned to face the attack, causing the lead German fighter to break off with smoke pouring from its engine. Whipping round in a quick turn, Baldwin then poured bullets into the second enemy aircraft, causing it to explode.

The third German seemed to have gone, but soon came back into sight, trying to get into the sun and so surprise Baldwin. Unperturbed, Baldwin climbed again to risk the hail of shot from the fast approaching Bf 109. The two fighters raced towards each other, firing their machine guns as the range closed. Both aircraft were badly damaged, but it was the German who baled out, Baldwin managing to nurse his aircraft home.

Now flying Typhoons armed with rockets, Baldwin and his squadron were given the task of attacking rail targets, such as marshalling yards, signal boxes, junctions, bridges and – Baldwin's particular favourite – trains. On just one mission, Baldwin found four locomotives, firing a pair of rockets at each with unerring aim. By the time he was awarded a Bar to his DFC in the run up to D-Day, his tally stood at nine German aircraft, 14 locomotives, six barges, a tanker and a tug, in addition to an exemplary record of shooting up rail junctions and other targets.

The more established airfields were still active, with Tangmere acting as a staging post for numerous squadrons coming into and out of the area. The Typhoons of No 266 (Rhodesia) Squadron were in residence for a while. Flying Officer Norham Lucas was lost to

A Typhoon prepares for a mission in the D-Day landings. The long-barrelled cannon protrude ominously from the wings.

anti-aircraft fire while firing rockets during a low pass, or so his comrades thought when he failed to form up after the attack. In fact his aircraft had been badly damaged, but not destroyed. At low altitude he managed to keep the engine running long enough to get over the Channel and find a patrol boat. He then baled out and was picked up, to get back to Tangmere that evening.

Meanwhile the Poles were still in action, attacking ground targets with their bombs and guns. Le Havre was attacked on 21 May 1944, Vacqueriette on 22 May and Douai on 24 May. Next day they hit Amiens, Criel on 27 May, Bavinche on 28 May, Abbeville on 29 May and Grenflos on 30 May.

The wing had a day off operations on 31 May to receive a visit from Leigh-Mallory and Sir Arthur Coningham. Thus far the squadrons had been operating only over occupied Europe, but it was confidently expected that at some point after D-Day they would get to within range of Germany itself. Naturally the Poles were keen to hit back at their enemy after their home country had been invaded, occupied and removed from the map. One of the Poles asked Coningham what the rules of engagement would be once over Germany. 'Oh,' came the reply, 'just shoot at anything you see.'

This remark by Coningham led to some heated debate among the Poles as to whether they were supposed to target civilian women and children as well as military and industrial targets. Coningham was forced to send a telegram next day to explain that he had meant that the pilots could attack any bridge, truck or railway that they saw, not just those they had been briefed to attack. He finished by writing, 'If you do see Frau Goering hanging out the washing, leave her to it while you concentrate on Fat Hermann.'

At 2 pm on 5 June 1944 armed guards were posted on the gates to all airfields in Sussex. Nobody was allowed to enter or leave under any

The wreckage of a Bf 109, one of the few German fighters that tried to intervene with the D-Day landings, is inspected a few days after it crashed down by a salvage team.

A squadron of Spitfires on an ALG prepares to take off for a sortie on D-Day. Note the bold black and white stripes around the fuselage. These were designed to avoid incidents of friendly fire.

circumstances. Soon after, the aircrews, groundcrews and others were all summoned to briefings. They were told that the invasion of Europe – D-Day – would take place the following day. The aircrews were given their missions, the ground crews told when to get the aircraft ready and with what weapons; the other staff were told when to cook meals, wash laundry and prepare for casualties. It was going to be a busy day and everything depended on each squadron being ready at precisely the right time. Nothing, not even a missing sock in the laundry, could get in the way.

By this time all Allied aircraft had been painted with bold black and white

Tanks rumble ashore on to Gold Beach on the day after D-Day. The success of Fighter Command in keeping German aircraft away from the landing beaches ensured that reinforcements and supplies could pour ashore in large quantities.

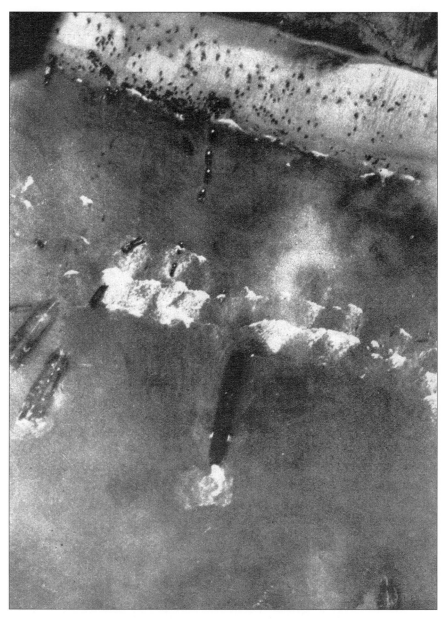

Gold Beach around mid-afternoon on D-Day as photographed by an RAF reconnaissance aircraft. The landing craft can be seen offshore while surf breaks over German obstacles. The dark dots on the beach are men and equipment.

stripes on the wings and fuselage so that they could be instantly recognised by other pilots, and by anti-aircraft gun crews on ships or the ground.

The combined forces of ADGB and 2nd TAF put up the largest and most extensive fighter force ever assembled. Flying to a carefully prepared schedule, the various squadrons went out to protect the vulnerable ships and landing craft from air attack. In the event, the Luftwaffe did not attempt any serious attacks. In part this was because Hitler was convinced that the main invasion would come at Calais and that the Normandy landings were an elaborate ruse to get him to divert German forces away from the real target.

Later, as it became clear that Normandy was the Allied invasion area, the Luftwaffe was ordered to attack. But by this date the once mighty Luftwaffe was not the force it had been. It was now outnumbered by the British and US air forces in Western Europe and was short of fuel and spares. The Luftwaffe was not, however, quite beaten. Pilot Officer Eustachy Lucyszyn of Chailey's Polish Wing found this out when his Spitfire was hit over Normandy on 19 June. He lost consciousness and woke up some hours later lying in a field surrounded by the wreckage of his aircraft.

Both Lucyszyn's legs were broken, so he stayed where he was for a while, assuming the crash would bring either French farmers or German soldiers to the scene. After several hours, nobody had turned up, so Lucyszyn began crawling towards a gate. When he reached the gate and had dragged himself through, he saw a sign indicating that the field he had just crossed was a minefield. It was now night and he slept. The next morning, still in agony, Lucyszyn continued across the next field. The effort took him all day. The next day he found some cows in a third field. When they ran off at the sight of him a boy came to investigate and found the badly wounded and dehydrated Lucyszyn.

The boy fetched two men who carried Lucyszyn to a farmhouse. There he was fed and watered while a local nurse was fetched to strap his broken legs to splints. Next day Lucyszyn glanced out of the window by his bed to see the farmer coming up the lane with two German soldiers. Lucyszyn assumed he had been betrayed, but it turned out that the soldiers were Poles who had been conscripted into the German army only to desert as soon as the Allies landed. They now put Lucyszyn on a stretcher and together the three Poles set out for the front line. They made contact with an American patrol, Lucyszyn speaking English on behalf of his new friends, and that evening they were shipped back to Britain.

Then, just a few weeks after D-Day, Hitler unleashed the first of his

Seen from an RAF aircraft, the sky over the south coast is filled with barrage balloons positioned at the correct height and location to stand a good chance of bringing down a V1.

vengeance weapons, the V1. This took the form of a pilotless aircraft packed with explosives and powered by a ram jet. The V1 was launched from a ramp pointing in approximately the right direction, and kept on course by a gyroscope. Range was controlled by the amount of fuel on board. The first trial launches were made on 13 June, then on 15 June more than 200 V1 flying bombs were launched. Over the next month

In an RAF publicity photo dating from July 1944, a pair of unidentified RAF pilots are congratulated for having shot down a V1 apiece.

4,261 were sent towards Britain.

To counter this new threat, Air Marshal Hill developed a three stage defence. Lined up along the coast was a string of anti-aircraft guns facing out to sea. These were to shoot down any V1s seen heading towards them, and all aircraft were warned to stay above 8,000 ft within three miles of the coast to avoid being shot at. Immediately behind the guns was a string of barrage balloons, trailing cables intended to entangle the incoming missiles. Behind the balloons were standing patrols of RAF fighters with orders to shoot down anything that got past the first two lines of defence.

Because of the high speed of the V1, there were only three fighters that could catch one: the new Spitfire Mk XIV, the Hawker Tempest and the American Mustang. Older versions of the Spitfire could attack if they dived for extra speed, but in a straight run they were unable to catch up. The usual method of dealing

A V1 races through the sky. The distinctive sound made by the engine was likened to a motorbike without an exhaust. When the sound was heard people would scan the skies for sight of the flying bomb.

with a V1 was to get behind it and open fire, hoping either to damage it and cause it to crash, or to explode it. This was dangerous work, for each V1 carried 1,800 lbs of explosives, and the blast could seriously damage or destroy the pursuing fighter.

It was a Sussex-based pilot, Flying Officer Ken Collier of Deanland's No 91 Squadron, who found a novel way of downing a V1. He flew his Spitfire Mk XIV alongside the flying bomb, carefully positioning his wingtip under that of the V1. By then lifting his wing, Collier nudged the V1 over on to its side and upset the gyroscopic guidance system. The V1 dived quickly into the ground.

A tragic hero of the battle against the V1 was Captain Jean Maridor of No 91 Squadron, flying out of Deanland. He had shot down eleven flying bombs when he spotted a V1 while on patrol. Diving down towards the V1 over Cranbrook in Kent, Maridor was seen to be chasing the flying bomb at high speed as it streaked over the small town. He then opened fire as the V1 was over open fields, but must have mistimed the attack. The V1 blew up, engulfing the fighter in fire and sending it crashing down in flames. Maridor was due to be married only four days later.

The vast majority of V1 bombs were launched from east of the Seine and aimed at London. As a result only the eastern part of Sussex came under their flight paths, with Friston and Deanland being used as bases for anti-V1 patrols.

Throughout June 1944 the airfields of Sussex were kept busy flying missions over to Normandy. Most of the 2nd TAF had been unable to move over to the Continent, as the Germans were keeping the invading armies pinned into a fairly small area between Caen and Cherbourg. It was not until 25 July that the Allies managed to break out. A British attack attracted the

A V1 is trundled towards its launch ramp by German soldiers. The sudden onslaught on Britain by this pilotless flying bomb came just days after D-Day.

attention of the Germans to Caen, then a US attack broke out at Avranches. Thereafter the liberation of France was swift. Orleans was captured on 17 August, Paris fell on 25 August and the Belgian border was crossed on 2 September.

The headlong rush could not be maintained as the Allies outran their supply lines and the Germans reorganised their defences. Nevertheless, it had been an astonishingly swift sweep through northern Europe. Significantly for Fighter Command, the entire strategic picture had been altered. No longer were there Luftwaffe bases just beyond the Channel, nor were there V1 launching ramps.

The brief respite was halted when Hitler unleashed his next secret weapon, the V2. This was a rocket carrying even more explosive than the V1. It was fired from sites in Germany to follow a high trajectory at supersonic speed. There was no fighter able to catch it, nor anti-aircraft

A V2 rocket takes off. The V2 flew so high and fast that the Allies had no effective defence against it. It was said colloquially in London that you could tell the difference between a V1 and V2 because while the former demolished a house, the latter demolished a street.

The Messerschmitt Me262 was the world's first operational jet fighter. It entered service in such small numbers – less than 200 saw combat – that it had a negligible impact on the war despite its startlingly advanced performance.

gun able to shoot it down. Hundreds of V2 rockets were to fall on Britain, causing great damage and loss of life, but there was nothing that the RAF's fighter pilots could do. It was an awesome weapon, against which the only defence was to defeat Germany.

In October 1944, the air defences of Britain were reorganised once more. The ADGB was disbanded and Fighter Command re-formed, with Air Marshal Hill continuing in command. The 2nd TAF remained in existence, but was now based at airfields on the Continent.

The Luftwaffe was by now concentrating on supporting the German army in its desperate defensive battles against the Allies on both Western and Eastern fronts. Apart from a few isolated night raids over eastern counties of England, the Luftwaffe was never again seen over Britain, and those raids were far from Sussex. On 8 May 1945 it was all over: Germany had surrendered. Although the war in the Pacific would continue, there was no longer any air threat to Britain.

Even before Germany surrendered, Fighter Command in Sussex was winding down. ALGs were being abandoned as no longer needed. Air Marshal Hill was given the task of planning the peace-time RAF, and his position in charge of Fighter Command given to Air Marshal Sir James

Robb, one of the most successful pilots of the First World War still flying.

In all, some 3,700 aircrew from Fighter Command had been killed during the war, plus another 1,200 seriously wounded and a further 600 captured. Many ground crew had been killed during Luftwaffe raids on airfields or through accidents. It was a high price to be paid for victory, but the alternative is unthinkable.

If Fighter Command had not been able to deny the Luftwaffe control of the air in 1940, then a German invasion of Britain would have been possible. And if the Germans had got ashore in any numbers the battered British army would almost certainly have been unable to repel them. Defeat would have been followed by occupation and a humiliating peace, leaving the two totalitarian states of Germany and Soviet Russia to dominate Europe. Whichever had won the inevitable war between the two, the future for Europe and Britain would have been bleak indeed.

The men of Fighter Command, whether they were pilots, mechanics, desk staff, searchlight operators or gunners, fought as a team. If the pilots have taken the lion's share of the glory in popular imagination, that is only just. It was they who had to strap themselves into their frail cockpits and go up to face overwhelming odds in the face of immediate death.

As Winston Churchill said: 'Never in the field of human conflict has so much been owed by so many to so few.'

The pilots' panel from the Battle of Britain monument in central London. This shows a group of fighter pilots racing to reach their aircraft in response to a scramble order.

Hawker Typhoon

Type:	Fighter-bomber
Engine:	1 x 2180 hp
	Napier Sabre II
Wingspan:	41 ft 7 in
Length:	31 ft 11 in
Height:	15 ft 3 in
Weight:	Empty 8840 lb
	Loaded 13,980 lb
Armament:	12 x .303 in machine
	guns or 4 x 20 mm
	cannon in wings,
	plus 2 x 500 lb bombs
	or 8 x 3 in rockets
	under wings.
Max speed:	412 mph
Ceiling:	31,800 ft
Range:	980 miles
Production:	3330

Big and heavy, the Hawker Typhoon could reach 412 mph with its enormously powerful Sabre engine, the first RAF aircraft able to do so. It made an immediate impact when it entered service.

The Typhoon was almost never built. The early prototypes all suffered from bent and warped airframes just in front of the tail when put through dogfight manoeuvres, and it was not until extensive changes had been introduced that the aircraft was safe to fly. When it entered service in the summer of 1942 pilots soon found that the Typhoon was hopelessly outclassed at high altitudes by German fighters, though it had the edge at under around 5000 feet. By 1943 the Typhoon – by now widely nicknamed the Tiffy – had become a dedicated ground attack aircraft. Its formidable hitting power and low-altitude performance made it superlative in this role. No less than 26 squadrons were equipped with Typhoons in time for D-Day in June 1944. It remained in production until November 1945.

Hawker Tempest

Type:	Fighter-bomber
Engine:	1 x 2180 hp Napier Sabre II
Wingspan:	41 ft
Length:	33 ft 8 in
Height:	16 ft 1 in
Weight:	Empty 9250 lb Loaded 13,640 lb
Armament:	4 x 20 mm cannon in wings, plus 2 x 1000 lb bombs or 8 x 60 lb rockets under wings.
Max speed:	392 mph
Ceiling:	36,000 ft
Range:	740 miles
Production:	1418

The Hawker Tempest was the last of the Hawker fighters to enter combat in the war. At low altitude this was the fastest Allied fighter in service, a fact its pilots used to good effect.

The Tempest grew out of the Typhoon, which it resembled in many ways. The key difference was related to the much thinner wing of the Tempest, intended to solve various airflow problems suffered by the Typhoon at high speed. The thinner wing meant that the fuel tanks had to be moved to the fuselage, which was lengthened to accommodate them. During its development the Tempest went through several different versions, so it was the Mk V which eventually entered service in April 1944. The Tempest was a better fighter than the Typhoon, and was its equal in ground attack. The Tempest remained in production after the war, but was soon replaced in front line tasks by jet aircraft.

189

Index

A

'ack ack', anti-aircraft guns 115–9, 120, 172, 183
Adamek, Flying Officer 175
Aitken, Squadron Leader the Hon. Max 29–30, 49
Apuldram (ALG) 14, 174

B

Bader, Wing Commander Douglas 132–5, 139–41, 142
Badger, Squadron Leader 43–4, 78
Baldwin, Air Vice Marshal Jack 152
Baldwin, Squadron Leader John 175–6
barrage balloons 41, 113–5, 119, 172, 182, 183
Bartley, Tony 52
Barwell, Flight Lieutenant Eric 114
Bathgate, Flying Officer Jimmy 167
Beaverbrook, Lord 29
Bentley Priory 7, 12, 114, 126
Bomber Command 30, 57, 131, 149, 152, 172
Boulton Paul Defiant 112, 114, 159
Boyd, Air Vice Marshal O. T. 114
Boyd, Flight Lieutenant Robert 62–5, 78
Bristol Beaufighter 54, 110–112, 114, 122–3, 125, 165
Bristol Blenheim 18, 21, 49–52, 54, 110, 112

C

Casson, Flight Lieutenant 'Buck' 138
Chailey (ALG) 14, 174–5
Churchill, Winston 23, 25, 31, 37, 81–2, 187
'circus' 131, 136–8, 156
Clarke, Sergeant William 165

Cleaver, Pilot Officer Gordon 67
Coastal Command 9, 151, 153
Collier, Pilot Officer Ken 183
Coolham (ALG) 14, 174–5
Cowdray Park (ALG) 174
Crowley-Milling, Denis 31–2

D

David, Wing Commander Dennis 80–81
de Havilland Mosquito 160–65
Deanland (ALG) 14, 174, 183–4
Desmond, Eugene 152
Distinguished Flying Cross 16–7, 29, 78, 80, 108, 144, 162, 164, 175
Distinguished Flying Medal 47, 68, 69, 112, 162, 164, 165
Distinguished Service Order 16, 144
Donaldson, Squadron Leader John 'Baldy' 69–70
Dornier Do 17 43, 50, 80, 87, 100–101, 112
Douglas, Air Marshal Sholto 110, 124–5, 132, 133
Dowding, Air Marshal Sir Hugh 7–9, 12, 15, 18, 22–3, 54, 79, 81, 84, 86, 109, 132
Dundas, Flight Lieutenant Hugh 135

E

Ensor, Flying Officer Philip 112, 162

F

Fiat CR42 'Falco' 103
Fighter Command 7, 12, 18, 57, 63, 76, 79, 82, 92, 95, 109, 112, 114–5, 126–7, 132, 135, 144, 155, 165, 171–2, 186–7
Fiske, Billy 79
flying formations 59–60, 135
Focke Wulf Fw 190 147–9, 154–5, 159, 172, 173
Ford 9, 14, 67, 112, 132, 164, 172
Franklin, Flight Sergeant William 47
Friston 9, 14, 184
Funtington 14, 174

G

Gabszewicz, Group Captain Alexsander 175
Gibbs, Squadron Leader Patrick 144–7
Gilbert, Squadron Leader Humphrey 152
Gloster Gladiator 18, 69, 80
Goddard, Flight Lieutenant Henry 111
Gossage, Air Vice Marshal E. 12, 22

H

Halahan, Squadron Leader P.J. 'Bull' 15, 17
Hallowes. Sergeant Herbert 67–9
Hawker Hurricane 7, 10, 13, 15, 18, 23, 26, 29, 31–2, 39, 43, 53, 58, 60–1, 63–7, 73–4, 79, 82, 86, 94, 96, 99, 105, 107, 108, 128, 131, 139
Hawker Tempest 183, 189
Hawker Typhoon 171–2, 175, 176, 188
Heinkel He 111 17, 19, 29, 32, 49, 52, 71, 80, 102, 114
Heinkel He 113 83–4
Hill, Air Marshal Sir Roderic 156, 183, 186
Hoare, Wing Commander Bertie 162
Hodges, Wing Commander Bob 167
Hope, Squadron Leader Sir Archibald 100

I

'intruder' missions 162, 164, 172

J

'Jim Crow' 131, 133
Johnson, Wing Commander 'Johnnie' 141–4
Junker Ju 87 'Stuka' 29, 39–42, 61, 63, 66
Junker Ju 88 49, 67, 100, 112, 134, 164, 169

K

Kenley 9, 102, 142

L

Langley, Sergeant Leonard 162
Leigh-Mallory, Air Vice Marshal Trafford 110, 124, 127, 132, 156, 164, 176
Little, Squadron Leader James 110
Lucas, Flying Officer Norham 176
Lucyszyn, Pilot Officer Eustachy 181
Luftwaffe 12, 18, 22, 26, 35, 47, 56, 71, 73–8, 83, 86, 90–91, 105, 108, 131, 181, 186

M

Maridor, Captain Jean 184
Marie-Claire line, the 166–7
McDowell, Sergeant Andrew 107
Messerschmitt Bf 109 18, 35, 41, 43, 47, 49, 50, 52, 56, 61, 65–7, 76, 79, 83–4, 86, 88–9, 94, 97, 99, 100, 102–3, 105, 133, 135, 136–8, 139, 140, 145, 152, 154–5, 156, 159, 172, 175, 176
Messerschmitt ME 110 29, 35, 39, 43, 49, 56, 63, 65, 77, 94–6, 104, 110, 159
Messerschmitt ME 262 186
Millington, Pilot Officer W.H. 85–6
Morane 406 18
Morgan, Flight Lieutenant 43–4

O

Observer Corps 12, 73, 92
Oxspring, Squadron Leader R. 151–2

P

Palmer, Sergeant Wilfred 156–9
Park, Air Vice Marshal Sir Keith 13, 22, 68
Pat Line, the 146–7
Peel, Squadron Leader 61, 63, 65–6
Pepper, Flying Officer George 164
Pile, General Sir Frederick 115, 120

Q

Quinn, Air Vice Marshal Sir Christopher 22

R

Radio Direction Finding (RDF) (radar) 12, 36, 48, 110–111, 115, 120, 151, 164
Raffels, Sergeant John 162
'ramrods' 131, 149, 156
'rhubarbs' 127, 136–8, 149, 156, 175
Roberts, Sergeant Peter 162
'rodeos' 127, 136–8, 156

S

Selsey (ALG) 14, 174
Sherrington, Sergeant Roy 162
Shoreham 9, 14, 67
Supermarine Spitfire 7, 18, 34, 52, 58, 65, 68, 73, 84, 85, 94, 105, 107–8, 125–6, 130–33, 135, 136–8, 140, 141, 142, 145, 148, 152, 154–5, 159, 166, 174, 175, 177, 181, 183

T

Tangmere 5, 7, 9, 13, 14, 18, 22, 26–7, 29, 30, 32, 39, 43, 48, 50, 61, 63, 66–7, 69, 78–80, 83–6, 96, 100, 107, 110, 114, 132, 133–5, 136–8, 139, 141, 142, 144, 151, 153, 159, 162, 165, 167, 173, 176
Thorney Island 9, 14, 67
Toone, Sergeant Joseph 164
Townsend, Flying Officer Peter 16–17
Tweed, Sergeant John 166–7

V

V1 'doodlebug' 182–4
V2 185–6
Verity, Group Captain Hugh 167–8
Vic formation 57–8, 61

W

Westhampnett 9, 14, 67, 69–70, 79, 86, 107, 132, 138, 141, 152, 156, 159, 173
Westland Lysander 144, 165, 167
Whall, Sergeant Basil 69–70
Woods Scawen, Pilot Officer 39–43

Squadrons

Air Defence Great Britain (ADGB) 172, 174, 181, 186
2nd Tactical Air Force 172, 174, 181, 184, 186

10 Group 12, 22, 64, 151
11 Group 12, 22, 68, 127, 153
12 Group 132

18 (Polish) Fighter Wing 174

1 13, 15
23 112, 162, 164
29 164
43 13, 17, 38–9, 43, 67
85 17
87 80
91 151, 183–3
92 17
145 61, 63, 65, 77, 96, 135
161 165
164 175
183 175
198 175
213 80
219 110, 112, 165
242 32, 133
264 114, 159
266 (Rhodesia) 176
267 69
501 102
515 159
601 26, 29, 80, 84
602 69–70, 107
609 64, 147, 175
610 133, 141
615 31–2
616 140, 141